Additional p  ... ... / ui ui

"The forces shaping world Christianity are multiracial, multicultural, and non-Western. *Future Faith* presents them in highly readable chapters, spanning every major short- and long-term trend. While the scope and content offer something for everyone, for white Christians in the United States, whether evangelical or (formerly) mainline, *Future Faith* is simply mandatory. Take, learn, discuss, and make plans."

Larry Rasmussen, Reinhold Niebuhr Professor Emeritus of Christian Ethics
Union Theological Seminary, New York

"A prophetic call to US churches to not only survive but also thrive, by consistently challenging the reader to look beyond their immediate horizons, geographically and ecclesiastically, through the creative and sometimes unfamiliar work of the Holy Spirit."

Wonsuk Ma, Distinguished Professor of World Christianity
Oral Roberts University

"A refreshingly new perspective on current developments, contours, and dynamics of world Christianity. The combination of real experiential narratives with solid academic evidence in the volume makes this work a truly remarkable one for the church, theologians, and ordinary readers with interest in the study of world Christianity today."

J. Kwabena Asamoah-Gyadu, Baëta-Grau Professor of African Christianity and Pentecostal Theology
Trinity Theological Seminary, Legon, Accra, Ghana

"Wesley Granberg-Michaelson's thoughtful, curious, and pastoral heart shines through in *Future Faith*. His wisdom and deep care for the universal church are clear. He throws his arms wide open, calling us toward inclusion and nudging us toward nuance. He urges us to faithfully reimagine what it means to witness to God's good news in an era of polarization and change. He summons us to love."

Jeff Chu
Author, *Does Jesus Really Love Me?*

Future Faith

Future Faith

Ten Challenges Reshaping
Christianity in the
21st Century

Wesley Granberg-Michaelson

Foreword by Soong-Chan Rah

Fortress Press

Minneapolis

FUTURE FAITH
Ten Challenges Reshaping Christianity in the 21st Century

Cover image: © Thinkstock 2017; Blank Dirty Grunge Wall by Shenki

Cover Design: Alisha Lofgren

Print ISBN: 978-1-5064-3344-8
Ebook ISBN: 978-1-5064-3819-1

The paper used in this publication meets the minimum requirements of American National Standard for Information Sciences—Permanence of Paper for Printed Library Materials, ANSI Z329, 48-1984.

Manufactured in the U.S.A.

To Jim Wallis, whose lifelong work has forged a
faithful Christian witness for our time
and whose enduring friendship is a cherished gift.

CONTENTS

FOREWORD

In the summer of 2016, our family visited Seoul, South Korea. My wife and I are naturalized US citizens who emigrated from South Korea to the United States when we were children. Neither of us had been back to Korea in several decades. It was the first trip to Korea for our two teenage children. One of the more intriguing aspects of our time in Korea involved engaging the Christian community. We met a Christian academic who had been influential in Korean politics, we met with the president of World Vision Korea, attended a packed worship service at Yoido Full Gospel Church, and met Christians from across the spectrum of life in the city of Seoul. Christianity can be encountered in a myriad of expressions throughout the country.

Our family has lived in Chicago for over a decade. On a typical Sunday, we have attended an African American megachurch, a multiethnic and multigenerational church comprised of fifteen different nationalities, and a Korean American congregation that welcomes an increasing number of Latino congregants. Both snapshots of our global and local ecclesial reality offer a hopefulness for the future church. They reveal a robust and vital

Christianity that has moved beyond a cultural captivity to Western and white Christianity. The future church is a present reality.

As this book by Wes Granberg-Michaelson will clearly reveal, there is a notable decline of Christianity in the West. This decline has also been most noticeable among white Christians. Simultaneously, there has been an explosion of the church in Africa, Asia, and Latin America along with the growth of Christian communities of color in North America. These counterprevailing trends have resulted in an acceleration of diversity on both a global and local scale. I noted these trends in *The Next Evangelicalism* (2008). I decried the cultural captivity of the American church but held out hope for the twenty-first-century church if the emerging diverse Christianity would be embraced. Now well into the twenty-first century, the picture of a diverse Christianity in the United States and throughout the world proves to be a challenge to many Western Christians. Instead of embracing the future church, American Christians may be threatened by the decline of Western white Christian greatness and supremacy.

These realities and the challenges they raise may be difficult to face. But they must be addressed. Many of us may choose to turn a deaf ear to this reality, but it will not stay hidden much longer. We need to hear these stories. We will not survive as a united Christian community moving forward into a new era of the Christian faith without engaging in these conversations.

I am thankful for my friend, colleague, mentor, and most importantly, fellow follower of Jesus, Wes Granberg-Michaelson, for offering this text to the church. A new reality requires a new vision. Because this Christian renewal movement is notably found outside of the Western world, it must be viewed through non-Western eyes. This experience of the Western gaze seeing the ecclesial realities through a non-Western perspective is severely lacking in our limited North American Christian experience.

Wes offers a thoughtful voice of integrity on this topic. He has traveled all over the world learning from the church around the globe. He has witnessed these changes firsthand and has discovered and experienced the move of God within them. He is a leader who genuinely loves the church, who has faithfully served the church, and who wants the church to flourish in the upcoming era. You may not agree with every conclusion he gestures toward, but that is what makes this book an important resource for conversation. In his attempt to bring truth to light, Wes offers a glimpse into a seasoned church veteran's journey into the future church. Will you listen to this story?

Soong-Chan Rah
Milton B. Engebretson Professor of Church Growth and
Evangelism, North Park Theological Seminary
Author of *The Next Evangelicalism* and *Prophetic Lament*

INTRODUCTION

Christianity is at a hinge point in its history. It's happened before, when major cultural, social, political, and theological forces have reshaped the practice and understandings of Christian faith in ways that have left an indelible historical mark. One thinks, for instance, of the conversion of Emperor Constantine in 312 CE and its dramatic aftereffects, or the East-West Schism of the global church in 1054. The Protestant Reformation, most often commemorated by the posting of the Ninety-Five Theses by Martin Luther in 1517, marked a decisive turn in Christianity, not only theologically but also with cultural, social, and political ramifications. We can also name the "discovery" of the New World, the Enlightenment, the scientific revolution, and colonialism as developments that precipitated dramatic changes in how those who confess Christianity practiced their faith and understood the world.

Today, Christianity is undergoing another major historical shift. For the first time in more than one thousand years, a majority of the world's Christians are living in the Global South. This trend is accelerating, constituting the most dramatic geographical shift in the history of Christianity. For four hundred years, Western culture shaped by the Enlightenment has been the comfortable home for the dominant expressions of Christianity in the world. Now all that is changing. Christianity has become predominantly a non-Western religion.

The demographic facts of this major geographic shift have been well documented and are now being more widely understood. But this shift is about far more than geography. The future of Christian faith in the world is being driven by diverse, expanding groups of believers centered in Africa, Latin America, and Asia. How they see the world and how they practice their faith are different from well-established forms of Christianity in the West. Moreover, in a globally interconnected world, and with the religious impact of migration, this shift is impacting the future of Christianity in the United States. That will only increase in the decades to come.

This book's purpose is to focus on how US congregations are challenged to change at this watershed moment in Christian history. I want to explore what this shift in world Christianity means for congregations, large and small, across the country. The words in this book are written for pastors, elders, deacons, seminary students, and others who are living out their faith in one of America's 350,000 congregations and honestly wondering what the future holds.

When I was at the beginning of my career, working as a young staff person in the US Senate, Alvin Toffler published *Future Shock*, a book identifying the dramatic but unrecognized changes created by the shift from an industrial to a postindustrial society. Then, in the next decade, John Naisbitt published *Mega-trends: Ten New Directions Transforming Our Lives.* It explored shifts happening in the worlds of business, technology, and politics that would impact the future, and it proved to be prophetic. Each had a profound and widespread impact.

Recalling both those books, I became convinced that a similar approach was needed to explain and explore what this shift in global Christianity means for the future of US congregations. This future is already impacting Christianity in the United States in ways that are often unnoticed and unappreciated. In this book, I have identified what I believe are the ten major trends, or challenges, that require our awareness if we wish to participate in changing expressions of Christian faith that are being driven, ultimately, by God's Spirit—that Spirit that is always shaping, molding, infusing, and renewing the church.

I bring to this book both careful research and a lifetime of experience. For seventeen years as general secretary of the Reformed Church in America, along with my colleagues I kept asking: What makes congregations tick? Why do some wither and others thrive? How are they revitalized? What are the challenges not even on their radar that congregations must face? Further, for more than thirty years, including throughout my service as general secretary and continuing to this day, I've been deeply exposed ecumenically to the life and witness of the world church. It's been my joy to interact with church leaders, pastors, and congregations in all parts of the world. And I have consistently asked them how are they living out their faith within their particular setting, settings often so different from those in the United States.

Moreover, it was my privilege to be a fellow at the John W. Kluge Center at the Library of Congress, where I was able to draw on its vast resources to research developments in world Christianity, including the religious impact of migration on US society and its congregations. From the providential gifts of this background, I've been asking, How will the historic shift in world Christianity impact US congregations? What are the challenges that we must face for the future?

Inviting Conversation and Change

This book, *Future Faith*, is the result. I hope and trust that it may start a conversation. It's designed with that in mind, so questions around each of the ten challenges are included to spark discussion in congregations, small groups, book clubs, or classes. While this is my attempt to outline the contours of future faith and necessary questions that we must engage, I'm certain that others may offer different perspectives and identify other questions. I welcome such exchange, because we need shared wisdom to decipher the shape of things to come.

Some global developments presenting external challenges to world Christianity are not addressed in this book. These include the rise of Islam, the persecution of Christians in some parts of the world, the growth of worldwide urbanization, the growing economic inequities in our globalized economy, and other trends. Considerable attention has been given to such questions elsewhere. This book's purpose, however, is different, focusing primarily on how the dramatic movement of world Christianity to non-Western cultures of the Global South present challenges and opportunities to the practice of faith in US congregations.

People often talk about "the view from thirty thousand feet." United Airlines credits me with flying two million miles, so I've had a lot of opportunity to gain such a perspective. Here's what I see. In most parts of the world, Christian faith is thriving, with new and vibrant expressions marked by surprising and unanticipated developments. Such changes are not without their own set of new problems, serious conflicts, and enormous complexities. But looking to the future, Christianity's global trajectory displays clear signs of vitality and promise.

Within the United States, however, as well as in Western Europe, the picture is different. Congregations often struggle, and established expressions of faith seem to be sputtering in the midst of rising secularity. The problem is compounded because most Christians in the United States instinctively believe that we are at the center of the Christian world. Realizing that we are not and embracing the re-centering of global Christianity as God's gift to the whole church open pathways for our renewal. We can choose to ignore the surging new realities of world Christianity, living in the theologically and culturally narcissistic isolation of an Americanized Christian bubble. Or we can open ourselves to face the challenges presented by the Spirit's movement in reshaping the global church at this hinge point of Christian history.

My hope and prayer is that individuals and faith communities will address these ten challenges as opportunities to embrace a new future reshaping Christianity in the twenty-first century. The prophet Isaiah said, "Behold, I am doing a new thing; now it springs forth, do you not perceive it?" (Isa 43:19 ESV). That is the fundamental question facing US congregations. It's now our opportunity to discern and welcome the new things God is already doing and discover these pathways promising renewal in our life together for the sake of this world, so loved by God.

1

■ CHALLENGE ONE ■

Revitalizing Withering Congregations

On a Sunday after Easter, my wife Karin and I were in Tucson, Arizona, and went to worship at a Lutheran congregation, one of nearly ten thousand belonging to the Evangelical Lutheran Church in America. A modern structure nestled among the hills on the prosperous north edge of town, with cacti blooming in its garden, the church was well positioned to thrive.

But the sanctuary was less than half filled, with that familiar prominence of gray hair, and there was only a handful of souls in the choir. A warm and thoughtful pastor, obviously committed to the life of this congregation, shared that the baptism of a young boy would be celebrated that day. Yet for the children's sermon, only that boy and a cute five-year-old girl with black glasses gathered to sit by the pastor in front of the pulpit. No other person under thirty was anywhere to be seen.

Announcements and prayers revealed all the good things that this faithful congregation was trying to do. A new partnership with the local YWCA was helping poor young women with their personal hygiene needs. Assistance was given monthly to a men's homeless shelter. Intercessory prayers were filled with a long list of members who were ill, hospitalized, or home bound, as well as the needs of the world. By the door as we exited worship, a collection plate invited donations to support the denomination's efforts combatting global hunger.

But, from the looks of it, this congregation is dying. It may well have another decade or two of enduring ministry, but for some years it's been burying more members than it's been welcoming, and these congregational actuarial tables don't lie. Their faith is genuine, their worship is true, and their life is marked by mutual love. But like the hundreds of cars that drive past the church each day without noticing, the broader culture is passing this congregation by. And they are not alone.

At the Kensington Hotel in Seoul Korea, across the street from the Yoido Full Gospel Church, the largest church in the world, I was discussing the future of Christianity with Scott Thumma. He directs the Hartford Institute for Religion Research, affiliated with Hartford Seminary in Connecticut, and we were in Korea for a conference on megachurches and global mission. He's one of the experts on religious life in America.

Thumma believes that 30–40 percent of congregations in the United States will close in the next thirty years. Most will be like the congregation Karin and I visited in Tucson. Such congregations have under one hundred members, with a higher percentage of those sixty-five and older and a lower percentage of those eighteen to forty-five than in the general population. As these congregations dip below seventy-five members and slip toward fifty, survival becomes an abiding preoccupation.

David Roozen, Scott Thumma's colleague at the Hartford Institute, has coordinated a comprehensive study of US congregations, with reports issued every five years. This Faith Communities Today study for 2015 discovered that for the first time in recent history, over half of US congregations—57.9 percent—had under one hundred members.[1] The question, of course, is whether this matters. I've heard countless pastors argue that faithful ministry, rather than numbers and growth, counts in the long run.

But numbers do make a difference. Roozen's survey shows that congregations with more than one hundred members show a greater likelihood of reporting "high spiritual vitality." For those under one hundred, less than 20 percent make such a statement.[2] Further, smaller congregations are far less likely to attract younger adults—as seen in the church we visited in Tucson. So, the downward spiral of an aging congregation intensifies.

These trends cut across denominational differences. Overall, the median weekend attendance at US congregations—the point at which an equal number of congregations are above and below this figure—fell from 105 in 2010 to 80 in 2015. Previously, evidence showed that historic "mainline" denominations had been declining since about 1965 while more evangelical and conservative churches were growing. But now the erosion of established, largely white congregations is seen among those groups as well. Even the Southern Baptist Convention, the largest Protestant body in the United States, has been declining in membership over the past few years.

"None of the Above" was an optional answer about religious affiliation on a 2015 survey, "America's Changing Religious Landscape," by the Pew Research Center.[3] This created a new category of people, labeled the "Nones." Pundits looking for fresh handles to describe religion in the United States loved it. This small piece of a comprehensive report quickly found its way onto NPR, *New York Times*, PBS, and other major media outlets.

Frankly, the narrative fit the biases of many doing the reporting: America is becoming less religious, especially among the young, or "millennials." Want to see the future religious landscape of the United States? Just go to Portland, Oregon, the green, sustainable mecca and world headquarters of Nike, where 42 percent of its residents are religiously "unaffiliated,"[4] a figure that is 10 percent more than either San Francisco or Seattle.

The actual statistics are these: from 2007 to 2014, the percentage of those in the United States claiming no religious affiliation rose from 16.1 percent to 22.8 percent, while in the same survey, Catholics, mainline Protestants, and evangelicals all showed declines.[5] And age clearly makes a difference. Among those sixty-five and older, only 11 percent admit to being religiously unaffiliated, while among millennials, aged eighteen to twenty-nine, 31 percent claim that label.

However, most of the "Nones" are not atheists, or even agnostics. Sixty-one percent say that they believe in God—a figure that has decreased but is still a majority. And about a third say that religion is important in their lives. It's from those seemingly contradictory beliefs that the term "spiritual but not religious" finds its point of reference. A growing number of people, especially those who are younger, are so alienated from established religious institutions that they won't identify with any religious category. Yet, many have active spiritual curiosity and interest.

> A growing number of people, especially those who are younger, are so alienated from established religious institutions that they won't identify with any religious category.

The overall decrease of young adults in the life of US congregations looms like a dark cloud over the future of established Christianity in America. Consider this: within the general US population, slightly more than 20 percent of people are between the ages of eighteen and thirty-four. Yet, only one congregation in ten reflects that similar percentage, much less any higher, within their membership.[6] That means 90 percent of US congregations have a demographic makeup that is older than the general population.

Further, the age of a congregation's members has a clear impact, statistically, on the likelihood of a congregation to grow. When examining congregations that grew by 2 percent over the past year, David Roozen's study found that almost 50 percent of those had less than a third of its membership comprised of seniors, over age sixty-five. And in those congregations where seniors comprised more than a third of the membership, only 36 percent grew by 2 percent or more.[7]

In the face of the growing religious alienation of a younger generation, along with aging congregations with decreasing spiritual vitality, the imperatives of congregational change are obvious. But this is not easy. About half of those in US congregations see the need for change to strengthen their vitality and viability but believe necessary steps are not being embraced or pursued significantly enough. Yet, as David Roozen's study points out, "In a rapidly changing world, thriving congregations are nearly ten times more likely to have changed themselves as are struggling congregations."[8]

So, the first challenge facing the future of Christianity, at least in the United States, is this: *Most congregations must change or face a slow but certain demographic death.*

All is not bleak in America's religious landscape. Returning to that conversation in Korea with Scott Thumma, we considered megachurches, which Thumma has studied in depth. More than 1,600 are now found the United States, gathering about six million people each week, or one person out of every ten likely to be in worship somewhere. They continue to grow, now often establishing "satellites" and becoming multisite congregations. Of these 1,600, 80 percent have a food pantry or soup kitchen, 59 percent are involved in job training, and more than half have programs for literacy and tutoring.[9] Most megachurches are laboratories of change; innovation is in their DNA.

Best estimates suggest that there are about 350,000 congregations in the United States. If Scott Thumma's predictions prove accurate, at least one in three is facing pressing issues of survival. Most of these are smaller congregations. Those congregations with 350 members or more have better chances to survive and thrive. And while these congregations number only about 10 percent of the total congregations in the United States, they include 50 percent of all those who worship on any given Sunday. Yet, no congregation is immune from the overall demographic challenges facing established Christianity in the United States.

What's Happening in Churches Outside the United States?

On the same Sunday in Korea, I worshipped at the largest Presbyterian Church in the world, Myungsung Church, and then at the Yoido Full Gospel Church. Both are in Seoul, and their stories stretch one's ecclesiological imagination. Started only thirty-six years ago, Myungsung Church now has one hundred thousand registered members. When I arrived at 6:30 a.m., the sanctuary was already full of activity. It was Children's Sunday, and scores of young boys and girls were rehearsing their parts for the service, which was to begin at 7:00 a.m. That would be the first of five services that Sunday.

Separate choirs of over five hundred singers with distinct orchestras perform at each of the services of Myungsung. Mission outreach extends throughout the world, but a special emphasis is also placed on humanitarian needs within Seoul and Korea. Rev. Dr. Kim Sam-whan, the founding pastor, carries an ecumenical commitment that is not always accepted among Korean churches. He was chair of the host committee welcoming the World Council of Churches Tenth Assembly, held in Busan, Korea, in late 2013.

Early morning prayer services were a feature of Myungsung's life from its beginning in what was then the outskirts of Seoul and continue to this day, drawing thousands. On my most recent visit, I joined their Morning Prayer Service on a Saturday at 6:00 a.m.; seven thousand were present, including children. About twenty-five new congregations have been planted by this church, and its global mission outreach stretches to over fifty nations. Included is the Myungsung Christian Medical Center, with its 169 hospital beds, founded in 2004 in Addis Ababa, Ethiopia.

Over breakfast with Rev. Kim Sam-whan and church leaders between the 7:00 a.m. and 9:00 a.m. Sunday services, we discussed the ecumenical challenges both within South Korea and beyond. Rev. Kim lamented how differences shouldn't lead to division. But in South Korea alone, there are an estimated 180 separate Presbyterian and Reformed denominations.

Later that day, I entered a Sunday service of the Yoido Full Gospel Church as Hillsong's "What the Lord Has Done for Me" was sung enthusiastically in Korean by thousands. The sanctuary holds eight thousand, but overflow rooms include thousands more, joining in seven services each Sunday. Satellite and internet links to other sites and congregations bring the total to about two hundred thousand. The church's registered membership now stands at 820,000. That Sunday's offering was devoted exclusively to relief for the victims of a recent earthquake in Nepal.

Like many indigenous Pentecostal congregations around the world, Yoido Full Gospel Church was started with ministry among the poor and marginalized, in this case in 1958 by Rev. Yonggi Cho and others. With just a handful meeting in a tent, Rev. Cho began preaching and practicing a message of hope and healing. Marked with charismatic gifts and blessings, the congregation steadily grew.

Today about five hundred pastors and five hundred staff carry out its ministry. Six hundred eighty-four missionaries have been sent to sixty-three countries. Within its own governing structure, Yoido has one thousand elders. Unlike many other megachurches and Christian organizations, where the founding leader eventually tries to pass control to a son or other family member, Yoido successfully navigated a change from its founder to Rev. Younghoon Lee in a process of selection guided by its elders.

The conference on global megachurches and mission Scott Thumma and I attended was hosted by a third such congregation in Korea, the Onnuri Community Church. Started in 1986, in thirty years it has grown to 111,000 members with 75,000 in attendance each Sunday. But Onnuri was founded out of a vision to be a local church singularly devoted to empowering global mission, developing and drawing on its own resources to do so. By 2015, it was fully supporting 854 missionaries in 70 countries, as well as its own publishing facility and global Christian TV network. The mission program of this single congregation is larger than the entire global mission efforts of several US denominations.

The stories of megachurches such as these in Korea are one of the dynamics shaping the growth of Christianity around the world. When those in the United States become focused on twenty-year-olds who would rather go to Starbucks than church, we easily lose sight of this broader global picture. In the same way that it's impossible to forecast the future of the US economy without understanding global economic trends, one can't fully grasp the challenges to Christianity in the United States without analyzing world Christianity.

Christianity is growing in Asia, even though Christians count for less than 10 percent of its population. In the last century, Christianity's growth was twice the rate of Asia's population growth. From its present 350 million, Christianity is projected to reach 460 million within Asia in less than ten years, by 2025. Korea has been one of the remarkable stories, with Christianity now including about one-third of the nation's population.

> In the last century, Christianity's growth was twice the rate of Asia's population growth.

China is the most unpredictable and potentially most influential country in charting Christianity's future in the continent.

Among both government sanctioned and "unofficial" churches, growth is rapid, undeniable, and often difficult to track. On any given Sunday, it's estimated that there are more Christians worshipping in congregations in China than in the United States. In contrast to American Christianity, many younger people in China are moving away from being "Nones"—those without any religious affiliation, reflecting the nation's Communist legacy—to becoming those who embrace religion.

The Atlas of Global Christianity by Todd Johnson and Kenneth Ross paints the most comprehensive picture of all the trends impacting the presence of Christians, and those of other faiths, in every corner of the globe.[10] One of ways they classify the world's religious loyalties is to keep track of those who don't identify with any religious faith, a number that is decreasing. They calculate that in 1970, 82 percent of the world's population adhered to some faith, which by 2010 had grown to 88 percent and is projected to reach 90 percent by 2020.[11] So despite the picture in Portland, Oregon, the world is, in fact, becoming more religious, not less.

That's dramatically evident in Africa. A century ago, only a few million Christians were found there, less than 10 percent of the population. Now that number has grown to about five hundred million, half of the continent's population, with 70 percent of them living in sub-Saharan Africa. This is one of the astonishing stories of modern Christian history. Today, one out of four Christians in the world is an African.

All this is making an impact on their societies. I've listened, for instance, to the story of Philippe Ouedraogo, a Pentecostal pastor in Burkina Faso. Seeing the needs of those who had dropped out of the formal educational system, he established an intensive program of education in the northern part of his country, reaching especially to children from ages nine to twelve. About two-thirds are girls. Now the success of this program is influencing the whole country's educational system.

Or take the example of Bishop Joshua Banda, pastor of a large Pentecostal congregation in Lusaka. Like many pastors in the continent, he began a comprehensive ministry to those with HIV/AIDS. It grew to include many other congregations, providing care for thirty thousand people. Now it is part of the Health Care Association of Zambia, which provides an estimated 50 percent of health care in that country.

Multiply stories like these by thousands of times and one can begin to imagine the impact of Christianity within the continent of Africa.

Latin America has a long history of Catholicism throughout the continent from the legacy of Spanish and Portuguese colonial rule. But in the last fifty years, Pentecostal and evangelical groups have been growing rapidly, at about three times the rate of Catholic growth. Projections have Latin America's Christian population reaching 640 million by 2025, about the same as that in Africa.

The impact of these developments on Christianity in the United States was illustrated when I attended a conference in Quito, Ecuador, between North American and Latin American church leaders on the themes faith, economy, and migration. I gave a presentation followed by an address given by an official of the Ecuadorian government, Julian Guaman Gualli, on immigration trends in his country.

Mr. Guaman Gualli was intent on talking with me after the session. He explained that he was from the indigenous population of Ecuador, tribal groups that have been traditionally located in the Andes as well as in the remote Amazonian regions of the country. In a famous story of martyrdom known throughout the evangelical world and beyond, in 1956 five US missionaries who attempted to establish relationships with one of these tribes in the Amazon were killed. Subsequently others, including the widow of one of those killed, continued their efforts, resulting eventually in many of those tribal groups converting to Christianity.

As with others from these indigenous communities, Mr. Guaman Gualli shared that he was a member of the evangelical church in Ecuador. With excitement, he told me that there were at least six churches from his own indigenous tribal group and others who had established "intercultural" congregations worshipping in New York and Chicago. The direction of mission, beginning with a legacy of martyrdom, had now been reversed.

> The direction of mission, beginning with a legacy of martyrdom, had now been reversed.

The astonishing developments in Christianity around the world are becoming present in US society through the movements of migration. About two-thirds of immigrants coming to the United States are Christians, bringing with them the vitality, texture, and expressions of faith formed in non-Western cultures. While often unrecognized and unappreciated, these Christian pilgrims are beginning to alter America's religious landscape in fresh and unexpected ways.

American churches tend to live with a narrative portraying society as becoming more secular and are losing the loyalties of their young people, who are rapidly exiting established churches. Further, congregations can't reverse the momentum of aging, and they struggle for the courage to change, hoping at least to survive, if not thrive.

The world is interconnected as never before. The irony is that the global narrative tells of a world becoming more religious, with Christianity experiencing dynamic growth and change that is bringing fresh spiritual vitality and relevant social impact. The question is whether US churches will be locked into a parochial story of their gradual demise or liberated by a global story that is bringing new life into its midst from unexpected places.

2

▪ CHALLENGE TWO ▪

Embracing the Color of the Future

Let's return to Portland, Oregon, with its thriving population of "Nones." It's one of my favorite cities. Former work
friends live there, and new church start pastors are doing pioneering work in this spiritual frontier. In terms of race, Portland is significantly less diverse than the nation. The African
American community in Portland is 6.3 percent, less than half
the national average. Its Hispanic population of 9.4 percent is
slightly above the country's average of 7.1 percent. This isn't all
that unusual for cities in the Northwest, and in fact, Portland is
far more racially diverse than the state of Oregon as a whole. Yet,
race may be a factor for its high percentage of those without any
religious affiliation.

It seems to be the case that when people talk about "Nones," they are talking mostly about whites. Not intentionally, of course. But I think this is a case of implicit racial bias. Just go to one of Portland's fabulous downtown coffee shops such as Floyd's, Barista, or Spella Caffe on a Sunday morning and look at who's sipping a latte instead of singing in church. They're mostly young, hip, urban, and white.

When the Pew Research Center identified the growth of "Nones" in its report on America's changing religious landscape, it also revealed how US Christians are becoming more racially and ethnically diverse. Moreover, pockets of growth and vitality among many different denominational groups are being driven by nonwhite believers. In some cases, this is dramatic, but journalistic coverage of the Pew report tended to overlook these findings.

Those in mainline Protestant churches steadily declined in number, from forty-one million in 2007 to thirty-six million in 2014 according to the Pew study. But during that same period, the percentage of nonwhites among those denominations increased from 9 percent to 14 percent.[1] It's a story I witnessed firsthand.

Beginning in 1994, I served as general secretary of the Reformed Church in America, the oldest ongoing Protestant denomination in the United States. It didn't take me long to figure out we were closing as many churches as we were starting, and each year our official records reported a decrease in membership. So, I worked with staff and the governing board to adopt a ten-year goal that included a dramatic increase in the number of new churches we would start.

Setting ambitious goals, even while encountering bureaucratic skepticism, was achievable. The more difficult task was actually planting many more new churches. We discovered that no plan to do so would succeed unless it was racially inclusive, reflected in the diversity of new congregations.

Like other mainline Protestant denominations, the Reformed Church in America was a predominantly white group, historically shaped by northern European immigration—in our case Dutch—with a small presence of other racial-ethnic groups, disproportionately far less than the general population. Further, we knew that a faithful witness in our society called us to address America's original sin of racism and to build greater racial diversity in our life.

> The more difficult task was actually planting many more new churches. We discovered that no plan to do so would succeed unless it was racially inclusive, reflected in the diversity of new congregations.

Decades earlier, the RCA had established distinct racial-ethnic councils. Later, we committed ourselves to antiracism training, instituted a new Commission on Race and Ethnicity, held summit meetings on "building a multiracial future," and increased the racial diversity of our staff. Then, for the first time in our recent history, we adopted a new confession of faith. The Belhar Confession came as a gift from the church in South Africa, born out of the struggle against apartheid, and declared that racial reconciliation, unity, and justice were essential dimensions of Christian faith.

All those steps were essential. But what changed the life of congregations on the ground and increased the racial diversity of the denomination was the racial composition of our new church starts. For the last several years, over 50 percent of all the denomination's new church starts have been non-Anglo communities of color or multiracial congregations. They've been established that way from the start. That's the way a multiracial future is being created.

As aging, largely white congregations—comprised overall of a middle- to upper-middle-class demographic with low birth rates—gradually decline, growth comes from new church starts. Since half of these are predominantly non-Anglo congregations, expanding racial diversity becomes a means of reversing, or at least slowing, trends of denominational decline. This has become a common story among America's predominantly white denominations, although some intentionally embrace this future, while others quietly resist it.

What I have learned from my experience is this: *Denominations across the religious landscape in the United States must embrace a multiracial future, with all the changes in power and participation that this necessitates, or they will dwindle as self-protective white minorities.*

Addressing Diversity

To the surprise of some, congregations comprising evangelical Protestantism in the United States, now totaling 55 percent of all Protestants, show greater racial diversity than their mainline counterparts. Beginning with 19 percent in 2007, by 2014 about one-quarter of American evangelicals were from nonwhite ethnic groups.[2] Importantly, this does not include the sixteen million members of historic black denominations in the United States, whose theology and preaching is often more evangelical in character but whose commitment to social justice and advocacy differs sharply from the views of a lingering majority of white evangelicals.

The Evangelical Covenant Church in America is an example of how intentional and focused denominational efforts can significantly alter the racial composition of its membership. Founded in 1885 by Swedish immigrants settling largely in the upper Midwest, the Covenant Church fit the stereotype of a lily-white group with an evangelical piety. But seeking a different racial future, its leaders became intentional in recruiting African American, Asian, and Hispanic pastoral leaders. This meant courageously addressing issues of racism and social justice as well as examining models of seminary training and ministerial formation.

The Covenant Church developed an approach to antiracism training called "Sankofa" journeys. A busload of participants, intentionally grouped in pairs of those from different races, journeyed to historic sites of the Civil Rights movement, such as Birmingham, Selma, Jackson, and Memphis. Intensive sharing throughout the trip, including interaction around key historical moments, created an experiential antiracism immersion on wheels that frequently changed attitudes and lives in fundamental ways. Over time, one thousand people from the Covenant Church have participated in such experiences. The Reformed Church in America and other groups have adopted the same strategy.

Glenn Palmberg, who served for ten years as president of the Evangelical Covenant Church, was convinced that the denomination's evangelical identity needed to be supplemented with clear biblical commitments to social justice and advocacy. Working hard to create a new department of "mercy, compassion, and justice," Palmberg knew that embracing a more "holistic" gospel was not only a truer expression of biblical faith but also essential to building a genuinely multiracial denomination.

Today the Evangelical Covenant Church is an outlier among US denominations, defying dominant trends. Each year it consistently grows in membership. In a forty-year period, it doubled in size. About half of its new churches are nonwhite. Beginning as an overwhelmingly white and largely Swedish group, now about one-quarter of all its congregations are non-Anglo, reflecting a racial and ethnic diversity that is becoming hardwired into its denominational culture.

Like any other denomination, the Covenant Church faces severe challenges. Recently it's been embroiled in a controversy over homosexuality, causing gifted pastors favoring a more inclusive approach to leave. However, although still a small denomination, the Covenant Church is demonstrating that an intentional commitment to confessing the sin of racism and to building a multiracial future is a pathway toward vitality in a religious landscape frequently described by narratives of decline.

Pentecostal denominations in the United States, it turns out, are among the most racially diverse. They also are among the few denominational groups that are growing. The Assemblies of God, for instance, grew from about half a million members in 1960 to over three million by 2011, increasing its membership six-fold in a time when mainline Protestant denominations steadily declined at rates of 25 percent to 50 percent. Key to that growth, especially recently, has been new nonwhite members, frequently the result of immigration. From 2004 to 2014, the Assembly of God's white membership decreased by 1.9 percent, while their congregations saw an increase of 43.2 percent in nonwhite participation.[3]

By 2014, 42 percent of those comprising the US Assemblies of God were nonwhite. Ethnic diversity is transforming the face of this major Pentecostal denomination in the United States. It's now poised to become a US denomination of over three million without a white majority, ahead of the curve in demographic trends reshaping all of US society. Other major, and formerly mostly white, Pentecostal denominations such as the Church of God (Cleveland, Tennessee) and the International Pentecostal Holiness Church show similar trends in their growth of both overall members and ethnic diversity within their US congregations.

Incredibly enough, those US denominations displaying the highest degree of ethnic diversity are the Seventh-Day Adventists and Jehovah's Witnesses. (It's interesting to note that the famed musician Prince, who died in 2016, grew up as a Seventh-Day Adventist and converted to become a devout Jehovah's Witness member.) Among Adventists, 37 percent are white, 32 percent African American, 15 percent Latino, 8 percent Asian, and the remaining 8 percent in other categories. For Jehovah's Witnesses, the statistics are similar except for a larger number of Latinos. At the other end of the scale of religious diversity among denominational groups are most of the mainline Protestants, including the Episcopal Church, the United Methodist Church, and the Evangelical Lutheran Church in America.[4] Despite their long-standing commitments to racial justice, they are among the least racially diverse religious groups in the United States.

At the same time, nonwhite racial-ethnic groups are becoming places of growth as well as fresh religious vitality within the changing US religious landscape.

So overall, here's the picture that emerges. White Protestants are in decline. From 1991 to 2014, their total number decreased by 33 percent.[5] That pattern will accelerate, simply because of demographics. Mainline denominations will be affected more deeply because their average age is older and they are less diverse than other Protestants. But this pattern will continue to impact all groups. At the same time, nonwhite racial-ethnic groups are becoming places of growth as well as fresh religious vitality within the changing US religious landscape.

Put simply, from the time of this nation's founding, a white Protestant majority, led primarily by men, has shaped and dominated America's religious culture, reinforced by a belief in white supremacy. Demographically, that is now coming to an end. In 2014, Protestants of all types were no longer a majority of the US population for the first time in history, dropping from 63 percent of the population to 48 percent.[6]

Of course, these massive shifts take time. And they mirror the larger demographic transitions going on within US society. Presently, looking just at race, a majority of children under five are nonwhite. But it will take until about 2042 for America to no longer have any dominant racial majority—becoming a "majority of minorities." This historic transition is certain. Consider this: Among all those in the United States who are sixty-five or older today, nearly two-thirds are either white Protestants, white Catholics, or white evangelicals. But among those who are eighteen to twenty-nine, white believers make up only 28 percent of that total group.[7]

Nonwhites Sustain US Catholicism

America's Catholic community is being transformed by its changing ethnic and racial composition as dramatically, and rapidly, as nearly any other part of the religious landscape. One simple statistic makes this clear. Among Catholics who are millennials, 52 percent are Hispanic. Further, the median age of Hispanic

Catholics is forty-two, while the median age of non-Hispanic Catholics is fifty-three. Up to 40 percent of Catholic adults in the United States now identify as Hispanic or Latinx.[8] This percentage will continue to grow as the overall Hispanic population in the United States doubles by the middle of the century. Since 1960, 71 percent of the growth in the US Catholic population has come from its Hispanic members.[9]

Last Easter, *The New Mexican*—the daily paper in my home town of Santa Fe, New Mexico—had as its front headline, "An Infusion of Faith." It told the story of the San Isidro Catholic Church in town, which had grown steadily from a modest congregation in 1982 to a membership of 2,800, with new families, mostly Latino, joining every week. This largely untold story is not just happening in that region but is being repeated in different forms throughout the country.

Hispanics, however, are not the only group propelling the growth of nonwhite Catholics, creating a thoroughly multiracial reality, and shaping the future of US Catholicism. By 2014, twenty-one million Catholics in the United States—about one-third of all Catholics—were born in another country. Although a large majority of these were Hispanic, it's important to remember that more than half of all US Hispanic Catholics were born in the United States.

The country sending the second most immigrants to the United States, after Mexico, is the Philippines, and the majority of these are Catholic. Similarly, Vietnamese and other Asian Catholic immigrants are adding to the ethnic diversity of US Catholicism and being reflected in the priesthood. Faced with the shortage of white Catholic priests, it's not uncommon today to find a Vietnamese priest serving a parish in West Virginia, or a Nigerian priest giving communion to Catholics in a hospital in Grand Rapids, Michigan.

Were it not for the growth of its nonwhite members, Catholicism in the United States would be in a precipitous decline. A host of serious challenges confront the Catholic Church—among them, for instance, is the fact that only 3 percent of US priests are Hispanic or Latino. But the demographic future of the largest single Christian group in the United States, totaling about sixty-five million believers, is being decisively reshaped by its nonwhite members. The question is whether its pastoral, social, and spiritual future can reflect the significant changes that this requires.

The ascendancy of nonwhite Christians among Catholic, evangelical, Pentecostal, and mainline Protestant churches in the United States doesn't mean that the rise of the "Nones" should be neglected, or that today's largely Anglo congregations will have no future. Far from it. In fact, there's a whole cottage industry of approaches and models to form Christian communities that welcome the spiritual curiosity but religious ambivalence of nonaffiliated millennials.

Emerging Churches among "Nones" and Millennials

Park Avenue in downtown Portland is true to its name—an actual park runs between its northbound and southbound lanes, as you'd expect in this green city. First Christian Church sits at the corner of Park and Columbia, three blocks from City Hall and two blocks from the Portland Art Museum. Within that building at 4:30 p.m. on Sunday afternoons, Christ's Church gathered for worship until it recently moved to a new location. It was designed to welcome those who may spend their mornings in nearby coffee shops.

Adam Phillips is the pastor of this new church start. Formerly he worked as manager of faith mobilization for the One Campaign, so occasionally you'll see pictures of Phillips and the musician Bono on Facebook. Phillips also spent time working in the Congo with World Vision. Ordained in the Evangelical Covenant Church in 2010, he and his wife Sarah moved to Portland in 2013 to start a downtown church appealing to the large number of the Rose City's "Nones."

Portland also has the second-highest percentage of LGBTQ residents of any metropolitan area in the country, surpassed only by San Francisco. For them, Portland is a welcoming and hospitable community. Christ's Church endeavors to be the same. Phillips knows that one of the main and well-documented factors driving millennials away from established churches is judgmental attitudes toward gays and lesbians.

Phillips didn't set out to establish a congregation to be a prophetic witness on LGBTQ issues. He simply wanted to plant a church that embodied the radical love of Jesus, and it organically became a welcoming and inclusive community. Starting any new church today is a demanding task, but Christ Church gradually grew.

However, a conflict developed between the church and its supporting denomination, the Evangelical Covenant Church, which was providing Phillips with his initial support and salary. The denomination did not have an open and affirming official policy toward LGBTQ people, and officials grew increasingly uncomfortable with the posture of Christ's Church and Phillips's leadership. After a series of painful conversations, the Evangelical Covenant Church withdrew its financial support. In February 2015, all this spilled to the media, first in Portland, and then quickly to NPR and national outlets.

Supported by his emerging and committed congregation, Phillips turned to crowdsourcing, using social media to find the financial support to replace what the Evangelical Covenant Church had withdrawn. Christ's Church website says, "We're a church that is hoping to be about the things that mattered for the ancients, and for us today. Looking to be part of a church community that is about faith and social justice, action and contemplation? Join us." Many are.

Christ's Church in Portland is one of hundreds of examples of new church starts and outreach ministries of some larger congregations aimed at inviting disaffected millennials into a life-giving faith community. Some of these are infused and nurtured by a loose movement often called the "emerging church." Searching for fresh and vital expressions of church that are free from both rigidly constructed doctrine and docile, predictable form, the emerging church movement has spawned collaborative networks of pastors and worshipping groups with global connections.

The movement spread widely, with enough influence to attract strong opponents as well. A Google search of "emerging church" today yields over two million results. Inspirational thought leaders and practitioners include Brian McLaren, Doug Pagitt, the late theologian Phyllis Tickle, and Tony Jones, among many others. Beginning in 2013, McLaren worked to link this growing network together through the Cana Initiative.

More recently, many drawn to this vision have become associated with "Convergence."[10] Its nature and goals are best described in its own words:

> The Convergence Network brings together innovative leaders from all streams of Christian faith to collaborate in the development of new ways of being Christian . . . new ways of doing theology and living biblically, new understandings and practices of mission, new kinds of faith communities, new approaches to worship and spiritual formation, new integrations and conversations and convergences and dreams. We are a network of over 10,000 faith communities, organizations and individuals who act together to create a more just and generous world.[11]

Of course, this network now reaches far beyond attempts to create forms of church appealing to the "Nones." But the commitment to challenge existing patterns of thought and structure, and to reconfigure the understanding of faith in a postmodern and post-Christian context, resonates deeply with millennials, as well as many others in the broader Christian world. And its impact on patterns of Christian thought and practice in the United States has been considerable.

When the emerging church movement was planting its grassroots, I was at the other end of the ecclesiastical spectrum, heading up the longest established Protestant denomination in the United States, which "emerged" in 1628. But leaders like Brian McLaren were more than willing to be partners in dialogue and exploration. We spent hours together, including memorable fly-fishing trips in Yellowstone Park with others, discussing the missional church, and Brian led a retreat with our senior staff and addressed our General Synod. Such interactions between the "emerging" and the historic expressions of the church were enormously helpful.

> But the commitment to challenge existing patterns of thought and structure, and to reconfigure the understanding of faith in a postmodern and post-Christian context, resonates deeply with millennials.

One of the issues frequently discussed about the emerging church movement is the extent of its racial diversity, or lack thereof. It's a question that its own thought leaders have directly engaged. In some ways, we're drawn back to the basic question about the "Nones"—how much is this a largely white phenomenon, and to what extent are efforts responding to this reality centered only in the progressive, white Christian community?

Congregations of Many Colors

The other emerging reality in the US religious landscape that often has gone unnoticed is the growth of multiracial congregations. The challenge of developing such congregations, defined by when at least 20 percent of the group is from a racial-ethnic background different from the majority, is arduous. Statistics compiled from national studies in 2008 indicated that of the estimated 350,000 congregations in the US, only about 7 percent met that definition of being multiracial.

But in recent years, the commitment to this vision of congregational life has deepened, with expanding resources, networks, conferences, and inspiring examples. Michael O. Emerson, one of the leading authors and researchers of multiracial congregations, has documented a marked increase in such congregations to 13.7 percent of US congregations. These congregations are now found blossoming from coast to coast.

Middle Collegiate Church sits on Second Avenue, between Sixth and Seventh Streets in Manhattan's East Village. Its roots go back to the founding of New York, when the city was first called New Amsterdam, and twelve Tiffany windows are illuminated in its present sanctuary. But its vision reaches to a multiracial future. Long embodying that reality, for the past decade Middle and its lead pastor, Rev. Jacqui Lewis, have hosted an annual conference bringing together pastors and practitioners working in multiracial contexts and advocating for justice.

In Santa Ana, California, a multiethnic, mainly younger group of hundreds gathers at "10Ten" (1010 17th St.) for worship at New Song. But this "church not bound by geography" also has worshipping communities in Thailand, India, Korea, Mexico City, London, and elsewhere in North America. Founded by Dave Gibbons in his living room in 1994 with seven people, the group became a megachurch in a decade with five thousand at its Easter service in 2005.

But Gibbons then turned onto a different path from formulaic megachurch success, moving to Thailand for a year and urging those drawn to New Song to move out of the protection of inner and outer walls and into the pain of others often on society's margins. They now call themselves "The Home for Misfits." Born in Korea, Gibbons's vision from the start was for a deeply multiracial ministry. That's reflected in their present team of twenty-two staff pictured with goofy mugshots on their website, including ten women and just two white males.

Between Dave Gibbons at New Song, with evangelical roots in California's Orange County, and Jacqui Lewis at Middle Collegiate, steeped in mainline progressive Protestantism in New York City's East Village, thousands of multiracial congregations now stretch across the country, growing in number and influence. They reach across the theological spectrum. Books, online resources, and conferences nurture these expressions. Mosaix, a network for multiethnic churches founded by Mark DeYmaz and George Yancey in 2004, is one example linking hundreds of these congregations, plus researchers and educators, together.

Still, America's churches are significantly behind the curve of the country's changing racial demographics. Author Soong-Chan Rah points out that using indexes of heterogeneity, public schools are found to be six times more diverse than the average

US congregation. As long as such disparities persist, a younger generation, in particular, will find it unnatural to participate in churches preaching a message of reconciliation and love with a membership far less racially diverse than the schools they attended.

But the racial composition of congregations is not just a matter of demography or a new form of sociological and spiritual correctness. It turns out that this is about religious vitality. Theologically, it's clear that God's Holy Spirit is most fully present amidst the full diversity of the body of Christ. That is central to the story of Pentecost in Acts 2 and the early church, crossing the cultural and racial boundaries between Jew and Greek, producing congregations such as the one in Antioch with dramatic racial and cultural diversity reflected in its leadership (see Acts 13:1–2). That congregation became the center of the gospel's missional impact extending throughout the Roman Empire.

> God's Holy Spirit is most fully present amidst the full diversity of the body of Christ.

Today, this is also true empirically. David Roozen's study, "American Congregations 2015: Thriving and Surviving," analyzed data from 4,436 congregations covering a broad denominational spectrum.[12] "Spiritual vitality" was a key dimension researched in the study, which attempted to define this term and relate it to other congregational characteristics. One striking finding was this: multiethnic congregations showed more spiritual vitality than their primarily white counterparts. Here's what the study said:

> Racial/ethnic congregations remain more energized than congregations in which a majority of its members are white whether looking at vitality or attendance growth.[13]

This important empirical observation shouldn't lead to simplistic conclusions, denying, for instance, the evident spirituality and vitality found in any number of primarily white and growing congregations. Findings like these are always matters of percentages and degrees. In this case, for instance, 43.3 percent of multiethnic congregations were found to have high vitality, contrasted to 24 percent of majority white congregations. Further, 53.6 percent of multiethnic congregations showed growth in attendance, compared to 29 percent of the mostly white congregations that have long predominated in the US religious landscape. Those percentages are almost 2 to 1 contrasts, revealing a significant difference.

What All This Means

So, what is the color of America's religious future? Clearly, white will no longer be dominant. In summary, here's the picture the previous statistics and stories have painted:

- Demographically, the changing face of America's church is hardwired into its future. Among all millennials, only 28 percent are whites who identify with some expression of Christian faith, compared to two-thirds of an older generation.

- Statistically, places of growth that are occurring within established denominations across the board in the United States—Catholic, evangelical, Pentecostal, and mainline Protestant—are being driven decisively by emerging nonwhite groups.
- Spiritually, multiethnic expressions of the church, increasing in number and influence, are more likely to exhibit vitality and growth.

The future church in North America will no longer be shaped, ruled, and controlled by the white Christian community and its largely male leadership, which has dominated its life since the nation's founding. The color of the future is multiracial, a reflection on America's shores of the thriving churches in Africa, Latin America, and Asia that are reshaping world Christianity. *The North American church must embrace the changing color of its future with a decisive shift in its dynamics of power or face a life as a dwindling white minority clinging to places of protective refuge.*

I love visiting Portland, Oregon. But I wouldn't go there to search for the shape and color of America's religious future. As I finish writing this chapter, I'm on a United Airlines flight from Chicago to Houston, Texas. It's a Friday evening, and every seat is full. Working men and women completing a hectic week are returning home, still focused on their computers. But also on board are younger Hispanic men and women, some speaking their mother tongue. A young African American man wearing a Braves baseball jersey intently reads a book. Nearby are two other black women with small children who now live in America but were clearly born in Africa, immigrating here some time ago.

When the plane lands, a smartly dressed Asian woman, in black slacks, a white blouse, and heals, with a bright red suitcase and black briefcase, both on wheels, and a leather backpack, gets ready to depart. In the terminal, I'm passed by two young men from India in an animated conversation with each other. Their language, I think, is Malayalam, spoken in the Indian state of Kerala, where 20 percent of the population is Christian. Boarding the Skyway car between terminals, the recorded announcement, of course, is in English and Spanish.

Houston is the destination for all, and most likely their home. It turns out that this sprawling city has become the most ethnically and racially diverse metropolitan area in the United States. Yes, Houston, Texas. The outreach of its diverse religious communities was demonstrated in the wake of Hurricane Harvey. It is places like this where one can begin to discover the color and vitality of America's religious future.

3

Seeing through
Non-Western Eyes

Entering Princeton Theological Seminary in 1967, I signed up for a course titled "Models of Missionary Theology." It was taught by Richard Shaull, who had been a missionary in Brazil and became a proponent of liberation theology before it had a name. (The term *liberation theology* was coined by Latin American theologian Gustavo Gutiérrez in 1971.) Shaull wanted his students to see Christian faith and theology through an entirely different set of eyes.

The reading list for the course was diverse and unexpected. Along with books by Frantz Fanon and Régis Debray, I purchased a copy of Thomas Kuhn's *The Structure of Scientific Revolutions*. The book, written only a few years before in 1962, had

43

caused a stir by challenging the common understandings of how scientific knowledge made progress.

Instead of proceeding in a normal progression, or straight line, of observation, research, discovery, and conclusion, Kuhn argued that scientific breakthroughs came when anomalies in a prevailing framework for understanding some part of perceived reality led to a new, creative projected vision or picture, which then reorganized existing data and experience in a radically fresh way. A chief example, among the many Kuhn offered, was the Copernican revolution, which first suggested a cosmology in which the earth and other planets revolved around the sun rather than the earth as the center.

Kuhn argued that it wasn't simple observation of facts but rather the noticing of anomalies, or inexplicable exceptions, in the prevailing way of understanding cosmology that led to a radically different and highly controversial proposed framework. It took further work by Galileo and Kepler to give credibility to this new picture, by making conjectures about the movement of objects and shape of orbits that fit with this alternative cosmology.

Kuhn described this process as changing the prevailing "paradigm." In fact, it was Thomas Kuhn's book that introduced the word "paradigm" into popular usage. Today, the language of "paradigm shift" is widespread and well understood. For instance, on the one hundredth anniversary of the National Park Service, I listened to a report on how its director, Jonathan Jarvis, described climate change as creating a "paradigm shift" for understanding the present and future of our national parks.

For Kuhn, a paradigm is a framework of understanding, with rules, models, and assumptions that organize how we interpret things we observe. More broadly, a paradigm is a way of thinking through what we understand as various parts of reality. It's like putting on a pair of glasses to reduce the blur, to make clearer sense out of what we see.

> A paradigm is like putting on a pair of glasses to reduce the blur, to make clearer sense out of what we see.

So why was Richard Shaull requiring this book as reading for a class on models of missionary theology fifty years ago? Shaull was taking Kuhn's theory, which related to science, and trying to apply it to how we understand theology, as well as sociology and economics. He was using the idea of a paradigm shift to introduce a radically new framework for how we read the Bible, develop theology, and think about social, economic, and political realities. As liberation theology developed, it originated the phrase of seeing all these realities "through the eyes of the poor."

Thomas Kuhn's original insight around paradigm shifts, applied more broadly, is a helpful way to describe what is happening within world Christianity. We have described the dramatic changes in where the majority of today's Christians now live. In 1980, for the first time in a thousand years, more Christians were living in the Global South than the Global North. That trend is rapidly accelerating. As churches continue to swell in Latin America, Africa, and Asia, by the end of this century 2.8 billion Christians are projected to be residing in the Global South, more than three times the number in North America and Europe.

But this change involves far more than just geography. Christianity has now become predominantly a non-Western religion. It is moving out of the cradle of Western culture and the Enlightenment, which shaped and formed most of Christian faith for the last four hundred years. This means a commonly accepted way of thinking, with rules, models, and assumptions governing how we observe and interpret reality, is changing in unanticipated ways. We're undergoing a major paradigm shift.

Volumes have been written academically about the overall movement of Western culture beyond the framework of the Enlightenment and modernity. The certainties of rationalism and objective truth within a secular framework of society, with an implicit faith in science and material progress, have all come under question and critique. This rise of "postmodernism," with its deconstructing hermeneutic of suspicion toward all frameworks of rational certainty, now has acquired, in many academic circles, its own certainty.

The critiques of modern secularism borne from the Enlightenment come from many sources. In philosophically informed religious circles, perhaps none has had more influence than Charles Taylor's *A Secular Age*.[1] In an 874-page award-winning volume, Taylor dissects the assumption that religion gets progressively "subtracted" in the evolution of modern, secular society. Instead, a "disenchanted" view of life is created that fails to comprehend human and social experience adequately. This calls for new "habits of the mind" that can appropriate enduring, diversifying expressions of religious life.

In various Christian intellectual circles, Taylor's work has attracted widespread attention, stimulating fresh dialogue over how to discern the often hidden and nearly unconscious assumptions framing the modern world. Taylor, a Roman Catholic, was even a keynote speaker at the Society of Pentecostal Studies annual meeting in 2017. His opus, which can seem intimidating to most readers, has been made far more accessible by James K. A. Smith's guidebook, *How (Not) to Be Secular: Reading Charles Taylor*.[2]

But the challenge is more than analyzing how religion continues to find unexpected places of expression within the prevailing, though evolving framework of secular Western culture, as important as that is. Rather, attention must be placed on the startling fact that world Christianity has now become a non-Western religion. Today, Christianity is experiencing its greatest growth and vitality in cultures that historically have not been framed by the Western Enlightenment and secular modernity. Thus, the theological development and cultural expressions of Christian faith shaping the future are occurring within a dramatically different paradigm for understanding reality. Comprehending and adjusting to this paradigm shift is crucial to the future of Christian faith throughout the world.

It's no easy task to outline this major paradigm shift, and attempts to do so here may certainly be judged by others as simplistic overgeneralizations. Yet, the fact is that a majority of the world's Christians today live in cultures where they put on a different set of glasses to view and interact with the world, in contrast to those worn over the past four hundred years by most Christians in modern Western culture.

A majority of the world's Christians today live in cultures where they put on a different set of glasses to view and interact with the world.

One of those voices who saw early on the importance and impact of this paradigm shift is Andrew Walls. A professor of missions from Great Britain, Walls has spent much of his career in Africa studying the forms of emerging Christianity in that continent and then contributing to the overall study and understanding of world Christianity. Lamin Sanneh, author and noted professor of history from Yale Divinity School, once described Walls as "one of the few scholars who saw that African Christianity was not just an exotic, curious phenomenon in an obscure part of the world, but that African Christianity might be the shape of things to come.³"

In describing how the framework for doing theology is dramatically shifting as Christianity has moved out of Western culture, Andrew Walls says this:

> The most striking feature of Christianity at the beginning of the third millennium is that it is predominantly a non-Western religion. . . . We have long been used to a Christian theology that was shaped by the interaction of Christian faith with Greek philosophy and Roman law. . . . These forms have become so familiar and

established that we have come to think of them as the normal and characteristic forms of Christianity. In the coming century we can expect an accelerated process of new development arising from Christian interaction with the ancient cultures of Africa and Asia, an interaction now in progress but with much further to go.[4]

Non-Western Lenses

So, what does seeing the world through a different set of lenses really look like? As examples, we can contrast in three ways how basic relationships and reality are seen one way in Western culture shaped by the Enlightenment, and another way in non-Western cultures.

Lens One: The Individual and Community

Enlightenment thought focused on the primacy of the individual in understanding the political, social, and economic order. The independent ego is the chief reality shaping a person. As modern political and economic theory developed, it placed the individual, with their rights and autonomous agency and authority, at the center of its systems. Naturally this extended to theology, with the focus placed on individual faith and the evangelical emphasis on one's personalized religious experience.

Non-Western cultures, on the other hand, often begin with the primacy of the community, stressing the values of belonging and mutual relationships. One's identity is firmly rooted in a tribe, clan, or extended family, rather than first of all as an autonomous individual. Communitarian impulses and a common belonging to the earth, or the web of creation, are the starting points for models of political, economic, and social systems. Religious faith, with both its traditions and belief structures, is almost impossible to comprehend apart from a shared community that also transcends barriers of time.

Lens Two: Rational and Supernatural Approaches to Knowledge

Western, Enlightenment culture placed a priority on the mind's ability to know truth through rational thought and inquiry. The scientific method became key to acquiring trustworthy knowledge. The mind became primary, echoed in Descartes's famous saying, "I think, therefore I am." Truth could be rationally proven.

Non-Western cultures often assume that supernatural forces, both good and evil, are the means that unlock knowledge of reality and truth. Insight into and contact with the nature of reality comes through legends and rituals, or dances and vision quests, which provide portals into spiritual realities upholding all life. Knowing truth through abstract thinking is a foreign concept in a world where one can touch reality through sacred lived experiences.

Lens Three: The Material and the Spiritual World

Enlightenment thought reinforced a clear boundary between the material and spiritual. What mattered was matter. With scientific discovery, it became all about atoms. The world was an object to be studied, analyzed, and then used, or exploited. Spiritual matters, including Christian faith, when acknowledged were usually circumscribed to a narrow, personalized domain and separated from the material world.

Cultures in the non-Western world typically assume a far more fluid and interconnected relationship between the material and the spiritual. Spiritual forces and realities, both good and evil, permeate the so-called material world. The origin and life of material objects are connected to spiritual forces. One's inner, personal encounter with spiritual life can't be secluded as individual experience but is interdependent with the outer "material" world and the basic elements of earth, air, fire, and water.

Of course, as mentioned, these are simplistic summaries. We know that colonialism created a complex and conflictive relationship between Western and non-Western cultures, with legacies that persist to this day. And in previous writing, I've tried to briefly explore the interactions between the legacy of the Enlightenment and non-Western cultures.[5]

But the point is this: for most of world Christianity, the movement out of the enduring, comfortable cradle of Western culture to the non-Western world entails a fundamental reorientation of how culture and faith interact in the process of theology around crucial issues involving how we understand truth and experience reality. In a Western culture, we tend to take for granted things like the primacy of the individual, the confidence in rational thinking, and the division between the material and the spiritual. Those are the glasses we wear. But in non-Western cultures, the lenses are different.

A Conversation in Akropong, Ghana

Across a table in a classroom at the Akrofi-Christaller Institute of Theology, Mission, and Culture in Akropong, Ghana, I discussed these matters directly with Andrew Walls. Then eighty, he was still sharp and engaged in teaching, lecturing, and writing on these questions, and he spent a morning with a group of us there for a committee meeting of the Global Christian Forum. The Akrofi-Christaller Institute has devoted itself to the development of indigenous African theology and is like a laboratory for exploring how fresh, non-Western paradigms shape and understand our practice of Christian faith.

Professor Walls explained that when Christianity was first confronted with the development of the Enlightenment in Western culture, it had to come to terms with that way of understanding reality, which erected a clear boundary between the material, or empirical, world and the spiritual world. Christian faith had to make sense within this framework, and spiritual matters were restricted to a personal or private domain that ultimately was protected from empirical, scientific "proof."

So, an important task of theologians in a world shaped by the Enlightenment was to "police" the boundary between the material and spiritual worlds, according to Walls. A space had to be carved out to protect the integrity of faith within a world where truth was known rationally and empirically. Miracles had to be explained as exceptions to the natural order or, in more liberal views, as the way various phenomena were interpreted "through the eyes of faith," as opposed to the prevailing eyes of reason and empirical verification.[6]

Non-Western cultures, including those in Africa where Walls had worked as well as cultures in Asia and other parts of the world, don't begin with a set of lenses that see a strict boundary between the material and spiritual world. So as Christian theology develops within these cultures, a framework that assumes the interaction of spiritual forces, both good and evil, within the "material" world is the starting point. This then impacts readings of the Bible and the understanding of the church's ministry in society. It shapes how Christians expect their faith to function in their lives and in the world.

Naturally, this doesn't settle or answer all the challenges to Christian faith and life. Rather, it describes the new framework, or paradigm, where theology is developed and faithful discipleship is explored. Further, there should be no attempt here to say that one paradigm is completely mistaken and should be discarded, and a new paradigm should be uncritically embraced as fully truthful. These are simply different ways in which Christian faith moves on its continuously incarnational journey, seeking to relate its truth to dramatically changing cultural contexts throughout the world. What makes this distinct is that presently we are in one of those "hinge points" in history as world Christianity in its emerging, dominant expressions is moving out of Western culture and becoming a non-Western religion.

Native American Lenses

We don't have to travel to Akropong, Ghana, to understand what it means to see the world through non-Western eyes. Revealing examples are found close to home, such as within Native American communities. The problem is that our nation's genocidal actions toward those communities historically not only decimated their cultures and population but often keeps their presence hidden, remote, and marginalized even today.

In 2010, the World Communion of Reformed Churches (WCRC) was formed at a global gathering held in Grand Rapids, Michigan. This new fellowship, comprising about eighty million Christians in the Reformed/Presbyterian tradition from around the world, united the historic World Alliance of Reformed Churches with the more conservative Reformed Ecumenical Council. As general secretary of the Reformed Church in America at the time, I was involved in negotiations for this merger and in the planning of the General Council in Grand Rapids, where all this would be launched.

An international planning committee was appointed to plan the program. Early on, its non-American members began emphasizing how they desired the General Council to have exposure to Native American communities as part of the way for Reformed Christians from around the world to understand the US context. Privately, I was highly skeptical. We were to meet in Grand Rapids, Michigan, after all, and not in Arizona. Its history was seen through the stories of Dutch immigrants. How were we supposed to provide these international delegates any familiarity with Native Americans?

But to be responsive to the planning committee's wishes, we began exploring what might be possible. It was to my personal shame that I and my local colleagues from the area's Reformed Churches discovered the active presence of Native American communities in western Michigan. We also learned more about their history, with the common stories of forced resettlement and genocidal persecution. That historical narrative, of course, had been largely ignored and suppressed in the accounts of the enterprising, pious, frugal, committed Dutch Christians who settled the area in the mid-nineteenth century.

When the delegates to the 2010 General Council convened on June 22, 2010, they were greeted on the banks of the Grand River near downtown Grand Rapids by Mike Peters of the Ottawa tribe with these words: "On behalf of the Three Fires Alliance and Native Americans from the four directions we want to welcome you officially and to celebrate with us in the spirit of unity." To the sound of sacred drums, officials of the WCRC were led in procession to Ah-Nab-Awen Park, a historical site where tribes originally gathered to trade.

George Heartwell, then mayor of Grand Rapids and a minister in the United Church of Christ, responded in remarks including these words: "Native American spirituality . . . teaches about one God, the Great Spirit, who is active in both the spiritual and material worlds." A Reformed worship service, led by Native American and Canadian First Nations people from churches belonging to the WCRC took place, followed by a powwow.

It took the coming of this international gathering of Reformed Christians from throughout the world to awaken those whose roots had been placed in the Dutch Reformed culture of western Michigan to the surviving and living non-Western culture of Native Americans in their midst. A series of workshops were held in the General Council, reminding delegates of how, in the words of Levi Rickert, a member of the Potawatomi tribe and previous director of the North American Indian Center in Grand Rapids, immigrants came to their land "with a gun in one hand and a Bible in the other." Mike Peters, who is also a pastor, held "talking circles" each evening outside the Van Noord Arena at Calvin College and blessed the delegates' meeting spaces with smoke from sweet grass.

On the first day of the General Council, the keynote address was given by Richard Twiss. A member of the Sicangu Lakota Oyate, Twiss was a noted author and educator before his untimely death in 2013. Having done a doctorate in missiology at Asbury Theological Seminary, Richard Twiss's ministry was particularly well-known in evangelical circles where he championed the recovery of Native American rituals, cultural practices, and identity while exposing and condemning the ways that missionary practices in American history destroyed native cultures.

His most well-known book at the time was *One Body, Many Tribes*.[7] In addition to explaining the history of how the Christian gospel came to his people wrapped in the covering of Western culture, destroying his own native identity, Twiss made a powerful evangelical argument for recovering Native American culture. Seeing Christianity through non-Western eyes becomes essential for interpreting the message of the gospel in all those settings and cultures free from the heritage of Western culture and for raising critiques about its limitations. Christian faith incarnated within Native American culture, in this view, becomes an effective example of vibrant spirituality free from the paradigm of Western culture and the Enlightenment.

After his death, Twiss's book *Rescuing the Gospel from the Cowboys: A Native American Expression of the Jesus Way* was published. Discussing the issues of contextualization in the book's preface, Twiss said, "There is an honest recognition of the guidance of Creator's Spirit behind the widening critique and correction to the hegemonic assumptions of modernity."[8] During Twiss's time at Asbury Seminary, when he was working on his doctorate later in his life, his critique of the gospel's captivity by Western culture deeply impacted international students

> Upon hearing him speak, seventy students from around the world said that for the first time, they felt welcomed in this country.

there. Upon hearing him speak, seventy students from around the world said that for the first time, they felt welcomed in this country.[9] That was the effect of interpreting the gospel through Twiss's non-Western eyes.

While Richard Twiss's writing and ministry had an impact particularly within the evangelical community and its ongoing debates around contextualization, a vast array of work has been done to understand and interpret Native American spirituality and religion as its own distinct tradition, with its worldviews and understanding of reality. One of the academic pioneers in that process was Joseph Epes Brown. For eight months he lived on the Oglala Sioux Reservation at Pine Ridge, and during that time Black Elk, the highly renowned holy man, basically dictated to Brown the meaning of his people's sacred rituals, which was published as *The Sacred Pipe*.[10]

Joseph Epes Brown was instrumental in establishing the academic study of Native American religion and spreading understanding of its worldviews and spiritual approaches to reality through his writings and speaking. In 1972 he went to the University of Montana to teach, where he remained until his death on his ranch in the Bitterroot Valley, south of Missoula, in 1990. His work served as a portal into understanding the interconnected, spiritually saturated view of reality intrinsic to Native American spirituality and in stark contrast to the outlook of Western Enlightenment thought.

Many writers have explored the relationship between Christianity and Native American religion. Kaitlin B. Curtice, a young Native American woman writer, has written a powerful account in her recent book *Glory Happening: Finding the Divine in Everyday Places*.[11] Jesuit Patrick Twohy's classic work *Finding a Way Home*[12] portrays the interaction of Catholic faith with Native beliefs born out of nearly four decades of life and ministry with tribal peoples in the Pacific Northwest. The reappraisal of and repentance for centuries of Catholic repression of Native Americans and their cultures within North America has been more clearly evident only in recent times. The Tekakwitha Conference now annually draws together hundreds of Native American Catholics to strengthen their distinct witness. It bears the name of Kateri Tekakwitha, the first Native American saint, canonized by Pope Benedict in 2012.

A personal journey from Grand Rapids, Michigan, to our new home in Santa Fe, New Mexico, has introduced me to a state where Native Americans comprise over 10 percent of the population, higher proportionally than any other state in the nation except Alaska. This amounts to nearly 220,000 people from twenty-three tribes, including nineteen separate Pueblos tribes, three tribes associated with the Apache Nation, and a large portion of the Navajo Nation. We have been immersed— at powwows, dances, art exhibitions, and rich historical sites— in refreshing opportunities to gain more personal exposure to cultures that frame their experience of the world sharply differently than those we unconsciously inherited from white, Western culture.

In summary, these indigenous cultures carry a profound belief in the interconnectedness of all life. The web of creation, in which we find life sustained by the Great Spirit, comes as a transcendent gift to be honored even as it gives life back to us. The material forms of life are but expressions of spiritual realities, and our calling is to maintain, or restore, the intended harmony and balance of the creation. Rituals of worship, prayer, dance, and art provide iconic manifestations of these realities and can be the arena where good and evil spiritual forces encounter one another and resolve their conflicts. One's belonging is shared to a wider community of clan, and then tribe, whose elders transmit wisdom and authority across generations. A cyclical pattern defines the web of creation and our life within it with spiritual connections that ultimately transcend the limitations of space and time.

Seeing through Non-Western Eyes

It's instructive to compare this to other non-Western cultures. For example, Christian philosopher John Mbiti, in his classic *African Religions and Philosophy*, writes of the different, nonlinear understanding of time, the manifestation of God in rituals, and the presence of divine "Spirits" as features within African religion. Spirituality seems to permeate African cultures in ways that make the Western, Enlightenment separation between the spiritual and the material worlds inexplicable to one wearing these non-Western lenses.

Comparisons between the huge diversity of non-Western ways of approaching reality and framing spiritual life are an endlessly fascinating task for students of religion. Further, the understanding and role of Christian faith within the diversity of non-Western cultures is the playing field for the most important theological work, in my view, in the twenty-first century. Whether one is committed to evangelical witness, Pentecostal growth, Catholic fidelity, social justice advocacy, or Orthodox vitality, all share a common agenda of discovering resonant and faithful expressions of Christian faith through the lenses and lived experiences of non-Western cultures.

In 1957, British philosopher Owen Barfield published *Saving the Appearances*, which would come to be regarded as a highly important work dealing with religion and the evolution of human thought. In only about two hundred pages, Barfield takes on the impressive task of chronicling the ways in which human thought and consciousness changed and progressed over the course of three thousand years. This includes insights on how our perceptions of the world evolve, changing our interactions with it and raising questions of what more fundamental reality lies beneath or beyond those perceptions.

Barfield contributes to understanding the paradigm shift from Western to non-Western cultures, and how this shift changes perceptions of the world. He refers to those in medieval times who assumed that objects in the world were related to a deeper reality in which they, as people, also participated. Thus, perceiving the world was also participating in the world—what Barfield called "original participation." Barfield's own words here are helpful:

> It is clear that [medieval man] did not feel himself iso-
> lated by his own skin from the world outside him to
> quite the same extent as we do. He was integrated or
> mortised into it, each different part of him being united
> to a different part of it by some invisible thread. In his
> relationship to his environment, the man of the middle
> ages was rather less like an island, rather more like an
> embryo, than we are.[13]

The paradigm of the Western Enlightenment assumed the clear separation between the individual as a subject and the world as an external, disconnected object. That framework, positing individual autonomy, objective rational inquiry as the gateway to truth, and the division between the material and the spiritual, became ingrained in modern consciousness. What Barfield describes as the medieval mind-set bears striking similarity to Native American frameworks for one's relationship with the world, as well as those in other non-Western cultures.

Barfield doesn't propose returning prior to the Enlightenment to "original participation," as if all that had evolved in modern consciousness with its detached thinking about the world never occurred. Rather, he speaks of a movement toward "final participation," which recovers the inherent though often unconscious connections undergirding the relationship between the person and the phenomena that they perceive. My own interpretation is that this means building on all that modernity in Western culture has taught us *about* the world, while retrieving our intrinsic connection *with* the world.

For most Christians in the United States, all this represents entirely new terrain. We don't recognize how thoroughly we've become trained to see the world through the eyes of the Western Enlightenment, with all its prevailing assumptions. This has become second nature to us, like wearing a pair of glasses for so long that you lose the awareness that you're depending on them. So, it's become natural for most of us to see and interpret Christian faith through this set of implicit assumptions.

An imperative of our journey is learning to see reality through non-Western eyes.

For the future of Christian faith, this will no longer work. *For*

Christians of all theological persuasions formed by modern Western culture, an imperative of our journey is learning to see reality through non-Western eyes. That is a required step if we wish to participate in the dramatic, unfolding story of world Christianity, bringing to it our own contribution and being enriched and changed by those shaping the future of Christian presence and witness around the globe.

In an interconnected world, numerous portals are available to help us try on a new set of lenses to view the world. Many are closer at hand than we have realized. Thomas Kuhn's metaphor of a changing paradigm, in my view, helps us see what's happening. Critiques of modern secularism provide helpful insight, but the lived experience of Native American communities, as well as the diverse non-Western cultures in Africa and Asia, with creative expressions of Christian faith within those contexts, all can serve to teach and enrich us. Numerous other examples can be found.

The truth is that the glasses of the Western Enlightenment that have framed our view of the world now obscure reality more than reveal it. We shouldn't simply be curious about how others see the world but rather seek to understand how our own vision has been distorted. We need corrective lenses for the sake of shaping a resilient and clear vision within our own culture in this time of dramatically shifting paradigms for understanding the world. That is part of the promise of embracing the future of Christianity as a non-Western religion.

4

■ CHALLENGE FOUR ■

Perceiving the World as Sacred

In the turbulent history of England in the seventeenth century, Puritans rose in influence and formed a coalition with the Scots in opposing the religious policies and actions of King Charles I. As the first English Civil War was beginning, rooted initially in a struggle over power between Parliament and the king, Parliament convened the Westminster Assembly in 1643. Comprised of 121 "Divines," or theologians, along with 30 members of Parliament, its purpose was to reform the Church of England, bringing it more in line with Calvinist and Presbyterian sentiments that had emerged from the Protestant Reformation.

The assembly met in Westminster Abbey 1,163 times between 1643 and 1649. Its most famous accomplishment was the Westminster Confession, as well as the Larger and Shorter

Westminster Catechisms. Their influence in shaping Presbyterian churches and denominations throughout the world continues to this day.

In its desire to reform all aspects of the church, including its government and worship, the assembly also produced the Westminster Directory for Public Worship. This document goes into considerable detail concerning how worship is to be conducted, including ways to use prayers before and after the sermon, specific instructions regarding the preaching of the word, how baptism and the Lord's Supper are to be celebrated, and even how to visit the sick, conduct marriages, and bury the dead. The entire directory was then adopted as an Act of the Parliament of Scotland on February 6, 1645, with instructions that it be placed in every church.

The end of the directory includes an appendix about the days and places for worship. And there we find this startling statement: "*As no place is capable of any holiness . . .*" [1] The point was to emphasize that no building for worship should be considered sacred or holy "under pretense of . . . consecration" [2] All this was part of the Reformation's rejection of those things "discovered to be vain, erroneous, superstitious, and idolatrous"[3] in the former worship and life of the church.

All the members of the Westminster Assembly were Calvinists. Similarly, the Scottish Parliament in the 1640s was controlled by Calvinistic followers of the Reformation. As such, they reflected the emerging mind-set and worldview seeking to "purify" the church (hence the term "Puritans") of rituals and practices deemed to be expressions of superstition and idolatry.

This reflected a legacy from certain streams of the Reformation that, in effect, separated spirit from matter.

One sees this reflected in the banishment of liturgical art in many of the Reformation's austere churches in northern Europe, with their blank walls and focal point on a high pulpit from which the word is preached. As Gregg Mast, Reformed historian and former president of New Brunswick Theological Seminary, has written, "Refusing to countenance a faith that had turned mystery into magic, the reformers drove a clear and decisive wedge between the world of spirit and the world of matter."[4]

This was most pronounced in Reformers such as Ulrich Zwingli, who saw no way in which sensible, material objects could hold the Spirit. Obviously, this all got played out in theological debates around the sacraments, and particularly the Eucharist. In the evangelical church in which I grew up, Welch's grape juice and Wonder Bread were never anything else, serving merely as "symbols" or reminders of Christ's body and blood, as Zwingli intended.

Calvin's actual views were more nuanced as he struggled to maintain the utter transcendence of God while acknowledging God's glory reflected in creation. Yet the Reformation's legacy of severing the Spirit from the material world was profound.

The Spirit's presence focused on the person and the people of God in worship, never on a place or the material world.[5] The result was a "disenchanted" world of nature, separated from its Creator, seen as corrupt because of the fall, and lacking any intrinsic value.

Then, on a related trajectory, Enlightenment thought emerged, spawning the modern scientific revolution. God was effectively being emptied from cosmology as the material world was regarded solely as a utilitarian object for study and exploitation. Francis Bacon, for instance, in pioneering the scientific method, spoke of how nature had to be "bound into service" and made a "slave."[6] Isaac Newton devised a totally mechanistic view of the universe, which functioned according to its own mathematical laws.

Likewise, John Locke, a devotee of the scientific method, grounded government in natural rights rather than any divine rights of a monarch and argued that nature was useless unless a person exercised labor to produce value, thus resulting in personal ownership. That understanding meshed well with the writings of Adam Smith, who developed a moral rationale for the pursuit of individual economic self-interest, dependent upon regarding the resources of nature as objects for utilitarian exploitation.

While this is only the briefest summary of the complex and even revolutionary patterns of thought and philosophy shaping the Enlightenment, the core reality was that modern thought constructed a view of nature and the material world that segregated it from God, except in the most remote sense. It's the meaning of what today is called modern secularism—namely, the attempt to construct an understanding of society and the world (including government, political life, economics, science, and culture) that is not dependent upon assuming the existence of God. But at its core, this means that nature loses any intrinsic value derived from its relationship to the Creator and instead acquires its value only through its usefulness to humanity, essentially as a commodity.

Thus, the philosophical framework of the Enlightenment and the scientific revolution transformed a sacred creation into secularized "nature." A vast, material storehouse of resources existed for the purpose of being exploited, inheriting value only through their utility. Applying the findings of science, human labor, and the tools of technology became the means to subjugate and expropriate nature in the service of human mastery.

A Perfect Storm

What transpired, then, was a perfect storm. From one direction, streams from the Reformation sought to purify faith by protecting the life of the Spirit from material contamination, detaching God's intrinsic presence from the material creation. From the other direction, the Enlightenment constructed a worldview that pushed God to the margins, leaving nature with value only through its usefulness to humanity's rule. The combination of these two movements acted like a whirlwind to empty the created world of any sacred significance.

Even more, the task of human labor in distilling value from nature took on its own importance as a religious calling. Max Weber, in 1904, described this in *The Protestant Ethic and the Spirit of Capitalism*. Discussing how Protestant "asceticism" ascribed a holy value to work, Weber said, "it not only deepened this idea most powerfully, it also created the force which was alone decisive for its effectiveness: the psychological sanction of it through the conception of this labour as a calling, as the best, often in the last analysis the only means of attaining the certainty of grace."[7]

Ideas and perceptions have consequences. Emptying creation of its intrinsic, sacred value, derived from the life of the Creator, now threatens the actual sustainability of the planet's life-supporting systems. Climate change is the most telling sign of this threat, signaling the impact of violating the integrity of creation through a mind-set perceiving only the utility of nature and justifying any means of its efficient exploitation. The crisis now threatening the planet's life-supporting capacity is without precedent since the advent of human history.

> Emptying creation of its intrinsic, sacred value, derived from the life of the Creator, now threatens the actual sustainability of the planet's life-supporting systems.

Larry Rasmussen, a foremost theologian and interpreter of our planet's plight, expresses where we are now with eloquence:

The eclipse of creation and the subjugation of life to capitalist imagination is also the eclipse of the sacred. The natural world as a community of kindred subjects and the bearer of mystery and spirit is nostalgia, if a memory at all. When everything is for sale, the numinous is leeched away like water from sand. Awe and wonder fade as the full drama of life in the natural world—death and renewal, birth and rebirth, life lost and emergent— eludes our waking hours. Rich though we be as consumers, as creatures who belong body and soul to the cosmos we are paupers.[8]

The captivity of biblical faith to modern Western culture has had few results more treacherous than imperiling the planet's intrinsic and sacred life-giving capacities. And while amplified by vast and overpowering economic and social forces embedded in modernity and the industrial revolution, the heart of the crisis lies in humanity's distorted relationship to the creation and its Creator. We take these damaging perspectives for granted, almost unconsciously, as the product of our parochial, self-serving understanding of the biblical witness and the view of "nature" that it produces.

But this has not always been so. Nor is the relationship between humanity and creation perceived in this way throughout much of the non-Western world, including those areas where Christianity is growing with explosive speed. The church that has dominated Western society, with its wedding to Enlightenment thought and the unforgiving capitalist exploitation of nature, now faces a task of theological reconstruction if it truly believes that "God so loved the world . . ." (John 3:16).

A Return to Ancient Theological Roots

Returning to its ancient theological roots is one place to begin. Inherited Western theology, with its evangelical roots, focused on the relationship between God and the individual. It is people who are saved by the redeeming work of Christ's death and resurrection. Salvation is directed toward humanity. This is the unquestioned starting point.

I never doubted this until I encountered theology from the Orthodox tradition, with its ancient roots in the church's earliest theologians. My entry point came through a modern Orthodox theologian, the late Paulos Mar Gregorios. When first exploring questions around the theology of creation and the environment, I came across his book *The Human Presence: An Orthodox View of Nature.*[9] In it he describes how Orthodox theology sees God's redemptive work as directed toward all creation and understands the intrinsic connection of humanity with creation, rather than detached from an objectified understanding of "nature."

Intrigued, I invited Gregorios to a conference on Christianity and environmental responsibility that I had been asked to organize at the Au Sable Institute of Environmental Studies, in Michigan. In the early 1980s, Au Sable was one of the few places anywhere giving attention to whether and why Christians should care for the earth. The lecture Gregorios gave at that conference left an imprint around Orthodox theological understandings that remains resonant to this day, more than three decades later.

Gregorios argued, first, that human redemption can only be understood as part of the redemption of the whole creation. He explained, "Both the Pauline and the Johannine witnesses in the New Testament strongly affirm this redemption of the whole creation—cosmic redemption, if you like, or the participation of all creation in the liberation of humanity from the bondage to sin and death."[10] Gregorios went on to say that "nature," as the stuff of the world existing independently of humanity and of God, is not a word that even exists in Hebrew or a concept found within the biblical witness.

In an Orthodox understanding, as explained by Gregorios, "the creative energy of God is the true being of all that is; matter is that spirit or energy in physical form. Therefore, we should regard our human environment as the energy of God in a form that is accessible to our senses."[11] Thus, Orthodox theology offers a theological framework for understanding creation, humanity, and redemption that is in sharp distinction from the familiar view of Western Christianity with its narrow personal focus amidst a backdrop of secularized nature.[12]

Such understandings of "cosmic" incarnation and redemption found expression in the Eastern church in early church fathers such as Gregory of Nyssa. Those voices were less prevalent in the Western church, but with some very prominent exceptions. Saint Francis of Assisi was most notable, of course, extolling the familial harmony—"Brother Sun, Sister Moon"—of creation's web as the embodiment of God's love. Saint Bonaventure, who followed Francis as a formative leader of the Franciscan order, described God as "within all things but not enclosed; outside all things but not excluded; above all things but not aloof; below all things but not debased. . . . [W]hose center is everywhere and whose circumference is nowhere."[13]

Such voices, also echoed in more recent theologians, found their most dramatic and resounding expression in the Catholic Church's first pope named after Saint Francis. His encyclical letter *Laudato Si'* (Praised Be) takes its name from the "Canticle of the Sun" by Saint Francis of Assisi, which praises God for the material world. Subtitled "On Care for Our Common Home," the encyclical of Pope Francis is a stunning theological declaration of the gift and intrinsic goodness of creation and a compelling call to address the growing injustice of global economic inequality and the alarming deterioration of the earth's ecological integrity as a single, interrelated challenge gravely threatening our future.

> The encyclical of Pope Francis is a stunning theological declaration of the gift and intrinsic goodness of creation.

Pope Francis clearly rejects the view of nature inherited from the Enlightenment and industrial revolution when he writes:

Modern anthropocentrism has paradoxically ended up prizing technical thought over reality, since "the technological mind sees nature as an insensate order, as a cold body of facts, as a mere 'given,' as an object of utility, as raw material to be hammered into useful shape; it views the cosmos similarly as mere 'space' into which objects can be thrown with complete indifference." The intrinsic dignity of the world is thus compromised.[14]

The encyclical argues that "the external deserts in the world are growing, because the internal deserts have become so vast."[15] So the fundamental changes in economic activity, political commitments, and international cooperation that are required must be accompanied by dramatic interior changes shaping discipleship. Regarding Christians who are indifferent to this crisis, Pope Francis says:

> What they all need is an "ecological conversion," whereby the effects of their encounter with Jesus Christ becomes evident in their relationship to the world around them. Living our vocation to be protectors of God's handiwork is essential to a life of virtue; it is not an optional or secondary aspect of our Christian experience.[16]

The encyclical closes with two prayers, including "A Christian Prayer in Union with Creation," which says in part, "Awaken our praise and thankfulness for every being you have made. Give us the grace to feel profoundly joined to everything that is."[17] Thus, the leader of half of the world's Christians, and the first pope from the Global South in over one thousand years, has declared that perceiving the material world with spiritual value, in contrast to the prevailing view of Western Enlightenment thought, is essential for the survival of our common home.

Contemplative Voices

Other Christian voices who have long apprehended the intrinsic connection between material and spiritual reality and have grasped the sacredness of all life are the mystics and contemplatives, both ancient and modern. It's remarkable how those called to an intense interior journey, often isolating themselves in caves or hermitages from the outside world, end up discovering God's presence permeating all things in a sacred canopy of infused love. Their detachment from "worldly" distractions in a journey of abandonment, seeking only God's presence, yields an experience of profound attachment to the beauty and harmony of God's creation. Hildegard of Bingen, Saint John of the Cross, Thomas Merton, and scores of others who were pioneers on the inward journey testify to the sanctification of the material world, transformed as the gift of God's creation.

Yet, in 1970, when the first Earth Day was celebrated on April 22, 1970, mobilizing an estimated twenty million people, the church seemed nowhere to be found. Despite the active engagement of many parts of the church in the Civil Rights struggle in the 1960s, and then in efforts opposing the Vietnam War, the coalition launching what became the modern environmental movement was remarkably secular. This reflected the widespread inattention of the Christian community to the theological and practical challenges posed by growing threats to the environment.

My own pilgrimage reflected this failure. Involved deeply in efforts to oppose the Vietnam War, working with evangelical, antiwar senator Mark O. Hatfield, and then joining Jim Wallis at *Sojourners* magazine when it was being established in Washington, DC, I was fully engaged in Christian social witness. But never on the environment. "Ecology," which seemed to be a new word, was barely understood. In this, I was representative of most Christians at the time, whether evangelical, liberal, Protestant, or Catholic, who were motivated by their faith to address pressing social and political issues of the day and to work for justice and peace.

Environmental issues only came into my awareness when my wife and I moved to Missoula, Montana, in 1980. There, environmental issues, such as the quality of water and the health of trout in the Clark Fork River, regularly made local headlines. The University of Montana had a well-regarded Environmental Studies Department, and the community was home to organizations and activists committed to saving the earth locally. But the church wasn't engaged. In fact, environmentalists often pointed a finger of blame at Christianity for its justification of the exploitation that was desecrating the environment through Christianity's injunctions to "subdue the earth."

Pilgrimages sometimes take one to unexpected places. In my case, I plunged into work exploring what Christian faith and the witness of the Bible actually said about our earthly home. What I discovered was that there wasn't much written—theologically—that addressed these questions. The vacuum, in fact, was startling. Charles Birch, a scientist from Australia, was raising these issues in ecumenical settings, and Paul Santmire, a Lutheran, was an early and lonely voice exploring ecological theology, writing

Brother Earth in 1970. But in the decade after the first Earth Day, bookshelves in Protestant and Catholic settings rarely contained such volumes. That's why the contribution of Orthodox theology was a refreshing discovery for those who, like me, were beginning to ask these questions.

Recovering the Integrity of Creation

The decades since then have witnessed a remarkable proliferation of theology accompanied by the growth of activism in churches and Christian organizations, which presents a striking and hopeful story. During the 1980s, as I tried to make my own contribution through writing books, articles, and public speaking,[18] I witnessed firsthand the rapid emergence of attention within Christian circles to the environmental crisis, both within the United States and globally. Multiple books began to be published at the intersection of Christianity and ecology.[19]

In 1987, five hundred people gathered at the Epworth Conference Center in northern Indiana for the North American Conference on Christianity and Ecology. Sixty-three groups and organizations sponsored this event, and participants included evangelicals, mainline Protestants, Orthodox, Catholics, and members of historic peace churches. Prominent Catholic voices were heard, including Father Thomas Berry, who had gained notoriety speaking of the "new story" of the universe. Wendell Berry, the farmer and writer, offered his poetic wisdom on restoring humanity's links to the good earth. This gathering, which showed the awakening of ecological awareness across the theological and denominational spectrum of American church life, could not have been imagined a decade earlier.

The next year, I was deeply exposed to the variety of approaches toward understanding and tending the gift of God's creation present in the global Christian community. In February 1988, snow covered the hillsides and roads in Granavollen, Norway, where two "sister churches" from the twelfth century mark the site where pilgrims stopped centuries ago, making their way to the Nidaros Cathedral in Trondheim, 533 kilometers to the north. But now, sixty ecumenical pilgrims from nineteen countries around the world were being gathered by the World Council of Churches to explore the meaning and mandate of protecting the "integrity of creation."

The impetus for the gathering came from the WCC Assembly held in Vancouver, Canada, in 1983, which adopted "a conciliar process of mutual commitment to justice, peace, and integrity of creation" as a central priority for its programs. Adding "integrity of creation" was innovative and intriguing, responding to the world's growing recognition of the environmental crisis. But what this meant theologically, and what might be expected from the WCC's member churches, was unclear. That's what those who gathered in wintery Granavollen, Norway, were expected to explain.

What stood out were the variety of global voices offering perspectives, experiences, and forms of spirituality differing sharply from dominant views shaped by the Enlightenment in

Western culture. Women theologians from the Global South shared views that had as their starting point an integrated understanding of the womb of creation and humanity's place of dependency within it rather than (male) dominance over it. Voices of indigenous people spoke of the picture of God's Spirit permeating and animating the physical world. Those traveling from the Pacific Islands shared how the changing climate threatened their actual existence. And Orthodox theologians, including Paulos Mar Gregorios, articulated how the incarnation of Jesus Christ had cosmic implications.

The gathering was a distillation of evolving understandings of the created world and humanity's role within it throughout world Christianity and beyond. Within the WCC, this consultation laid the foundation for its commitment to mobilize churches in combatting climate change, a process begun with prescient commitment in 1990 that has continued to this day. Fresh theological work continued to grow, such as Sallie McFague's *The Body of God: An Ecological Theology*.[20] More broadly, the challenge of ecological sustainability, captured by the imaginative phrase "integrity of creation," became firmly rooted in the work of churches and ecumenical communities throughout the world in the past twenty-five years.

Such commitment is not confined to the ecumenical segment of world Christianity. Evangelicals have been embracing commitments to protect and preserve the earth. The World Evangelical Alliance, a network of churches and national evangelical organizations in 129 nations, formed a "Creation Care Task Force" with members around the globe. Its description states, "Throughout the world evangelical Christians are becoming increasingly aware of the biblical mandate to properly care for the gift of creation God entrusted to humankind. . . . Evangelicals are increasingly aware that creation care is a matter of biblical justice." Its goals are to equip leaders, mobilize organizations, and engage governments for these purposes.

The Orthodox Church, in addition to its theological contributions within the ecumenical community and beyond, has offered decisive leadership on environmental questions through its ecumenical patriarch Bartholomew. In addition to powerful declarations, he has gathered scientists, politicians, and church leaders in pivotal places around the world that are confronting threats to water quality, and frequently convenes conferences on environmental issues, emphasizing humanity's capacity for sin against God's creation. Through this work, Bartholomew has become known as the "Green Patriarch," as he has tirelessly tried to provide an example of such leadership from the Orthodox community.

> Evangelicals are increasingly aware that creation care is a matter of biblical justice.

In many respects, *Laudato Si'*, the encyclical of Pope Francis, represents the culmination of ecological theology as it has developed over the past three decades. It didn't just emerge out of thin air now contaminated with excess carbon. In fact, the encyclical would have been impossible to imagine without all the preceding, probing theological attentiveness to creation's peril.

A Sacred World

From a Christian perspective, the doctrine of the incarnation provides the most compelling demonstration of the integral unity between the spiritual and material dimensions of creation. Franciscan theologian Richard Rohr, who heads the Center for Action and Contemplation in Albuquerque, New Mexico, explains how early theologians from the Eastern church understood that "Jesus is the union of human and divine in space and time, and the Christ is the eternal union of matter and Spirit from the beginning of time."[21] The Franciscan sister and scientist Ilia Delio puts it this way:

> Christ invests himself organically within all creation, immersing himself in things, in the heart of matter, and thus unifying the world. The universe is physically impregnated to the very core of its matter by the influence of his superhuman nature. Everything is physically "christified," gathered up by the incarnate Word as nourishment that assimilates, transforms, and divinizes.[22]

The radical implications of the incarnation for understanding the material and spiritual worlds never seemed to enter the minds of the Calvinists who met over one thousand times in Westminster Cathedral, and that vacuum continues for most modern, Western Christians. As we approach the fiftieth anniversary of the first Earth Day, however, fresh understandings have been steadily and persistently emerging. One can say there's been a sea change in the transformation of modern Christian views of God's creation.

But the seas continue to change, rapidly. And while book-shelves are now full of rich works that theologically reconstruct the interrelationship of God, humanity, and the rest of creation, economic forces seem to grind on, still regarding "nature" as a slave to be held in human mastery. Climate change deniers, whose numbers now could barely fill a large rowboat on rising seas, nev-ertheless are ascendant in political power in the world's most powerful economy. And eight out of ten white evangelicals voted for the president who championed this scientifically lost cause.

The church where I worship, United Church of Santa Fe, receives all its electrical power from the sun, via solar panels blessed with prayers. It's inspiring and feels spiritually and mate-rially integrated. And our congregation is not alone. Interfaith Power and Light, devoted to encouraging and connecting con-gregations as models of effective environmental stewardship, now has twenty thousand congregations involved with chapters in forty states. Yet congregations like these comprise less than 10 percent of the 350,000 congregations across the United States. Most remain captive to unchanging mind-sets that keep God separate from the material reality of the world, even while that cultural mind-set allows the world's environment to be changed in such perilous ways.

Therefore, Christianity must once again learn to perceive a sacred world. And then that inspired vision, with ancient roots and growing expressions, must be given concrete form in ways that can transform the economic and political systems that so forcefully disregard and degrade the gift of God's creation. It is a long way from declaring that "no place is capable of any holiness" to perceiving the world as God's cathedral. But that journey is indispensable for our future. If Christians are not on that path, they not only are forsaking the God they claim to worship, they will also be forsaken by growing millions who cannot conceive of a God who does not desire to save the world.

5

Affirming Spirit-Filled Communities

I had never heard of Christine Caine. But I'll always remember her. She was the first woman to address the crowd of five thousand Pentecostals from seventy nations in the program of Empowered21, at the Pais Arena in Jerusalem. Caine followed eight men who had already preached at this event, taking place over Pentecost in May 2015. Its organizers claimed it was the largest, most geographically diverse group of Christians to gather in Jerusalem over Pentecost since the first such gathering recorded in Acts 2, where thousands experienced the outpouring of God's Holy Spirit. Those making a pilgrimage to Jerusalem two thousand years later were seeking a repeat performance.

Caine gave a passionate and prophetic call for the church to be continually changing, even while at its core it is "the same."

That constant change is driven by God's continuing call to be sent as witnesses in the world. "We want power," she told the spiritually hungry Pentecostals gathered before her. "But we don't know what it's for." She insisted that it's not for ourselves or for our own spiritual ecstasy. The power of God's Spirit is given for us to be witnesses to God's transforming love. And one can't change the world without being in the world, instead of running from it. "We're not here," Christine Caine proclaimed, "to entertain ourselves."

Coming after emotionally enthused Pentecostal preaching and praise, backed up by high octane praise music with pulsating strobe lights, her words seemed almost like an admonishment, striking a deep cord within the crowd of those listening. I walked over to sit by a friend who is bishop of a large Pentecostal Church. "This is the best word that's been spoken," he said to me. And that's after we had heard world-famous Pentecostal preachers.

Christine Caine is the cofounder, with her husband, of the A21 Campaign, an anti-human-trafficking organization fighting slavery around the world. Her roots are in Australia's Hillsong Church, which has spawned megachurches around the globe and whose music has saturated worship throughout the Christian world. She was just one of a plethora of speakers and workshop leaders from the diversity of the growing Pentecostal world who had come to Jerusalem during those days.

Another was Rev. Enoch A. Adeboye, leader of the Redeemed Christian Church of God. Founded as a single congregation in Nigeria in 1952, this "denomination" has moved with African migration around the world and now is present in 192 nations, including over 700 congregations in the United States. Unlike other famous Pentecostal preachers at Empowered21, Adeboye's preaching style was straightforward, restrained, clear, and direct. He stressed the making of disciples, also testifying to God's healing power.

In the United States, his church has built a worship pavilion north of Dallas for $15 million, which holds ten thousand. But in Nigeria each year he convenes the "Holy Ghost Conference." There, four million people come, and a covering has been constructed that is one mile long and a half mile wide to hold them. I am not making this up. Yoido Full Gospel Church in South Korea, described in chapter 1, is the world's largest single church, with over eight hundred thousand members. But the Redeemed Christian Church of God in Nigeria hosts the largest Christian gathering in the world. It rivaled the number of people who showed up in Chicago when the Cubs won the World Series in 2016.

The Rise of Pentecostalism

Pentecostalism is spreading throughout the world like a spiritual tsunami. Its growth is one of the most dramatic developments in the last century of Christian history. Modern Pentecostalism's beginning, at least in the United States, is usually dated to the Azusa Street Revival in Los Angeles a little more than a century ago, in 1906. By 1970, Pentecostals (including charismatics in non-Pentecostal denominations) totaled about sixty-two million, or only 5 percent of the total Christian population. But in the four decades that followed, Pentecostalism grew at four times the rate of all Christianity, and four times faster than overall world population growth.

Today, Pentecostals number at least six hundred million, ten times their number in 1970. One out of every four Christians in the world is Pentecostal or charismatic. One of four Pentecostals is an Asian, and 80 percent of Christian conversions in Asia are to Pentecostal forms of Christianity. One out of three Pentecostals is in Africa. In Latin America, Pentecostalism is growing at three times the rate of Catholicism.

> One out of every four Christians in the world is Pentecostal or charismatic.

Think of it this way. One out of every twelve people alive in the world today is Pentecostal. For a movement generally regarded as only about a century old, this is an astonishing religious development.

The one hundredth anniversary of the Azusa Street Revival was celebrated with a gathering of thousands of Pentecostals in Los Angeles in April 2006. I was invited to be part of a small delegation from the World Council of Churches to observe this occasion through the hospitality of Bishop James Leggett, then president of the Pentecostal World Fellowship. It proved to be a deep and moving ecumenical learning experience.

During that time, the history of the formative Azusa Street Revival was remembered with the help of noted Pentecostal historians such as Cecil "Mel" Robeck Jr. from Fuller Seminary. The movement began in 1906 with the preaching of a thirty-five-year-old black pastor, William Seymour. As people began to speak in tongues, crowds grew until thousands were worshipping in services held three times a day, seven days a week, continuing for three years. Reflecting the racial and cultural diversity of the first Pentecost, those participating included Hispanics, Asians, blacks, and whites, drawing from the immigrant population in Los Angeles.[1]

Since that humble beginning, Pentecostalism has charted a course as unpredictable and surprising as its inception. As the movement became institutionalized in American Pentecostal denominations, however, it also became segregated. More recently, as noted in chapter 2, increasing racial diversity largely from immigrant communities is driving growth in formerly mostly white denominations like the Assemblies of God and the Church of God. But television has also shaped the modern image of Pentecostals through successful preachers who often extol versions of the "prosperity gospel" and find favor from President Donald Trump.

Yet, Pentecostalism's most formative contemporary stories are found outside of the United States. Throughout the Global South, Pentecostal communities frequently arise among those on the margins of society. The poor and displaced, often disregarded and discarded by their societies, find a holy affirmation of their self-worth and a sense of personal and social empowerment through the Pentecostal communities that are born and grow in their midst.

Pentecostalism and the Marginalized

In 2013, I journeyed to Kuala Lumpur, Malaysia, to attend the Twenty-Third Pentecostal World Conference, an event occurring every three years in different parts of the globe. Over three thousand pastors, leaders, and youth came from seventy-three countries around the world. Nightly plenary sessions that were more like revival services, always with powerful preachers and dynamic contemporary worship, highlighted the time. I had come as a warmly welcomed guest, and I particularly wanted to explore the how Pentecostals regarded social action around issues of justice.

Among a series of diverse workshops, I went to one focused on Pentecostalism, social engagement, and justice. There, Ivan Satyavrata, who heads an Assemblies of God ministry in Kolkata (Calcutta), India, presented a talk titled "Power to the Poor: The Pentecostal Tradition of Social Engagement." Part of his thesis was that "the extraordinary success of the Pentecostal movement is largely due to its reach to those on the periphery of society."

Satyavrata argued persuasively from history that early Pentecostalism had a deep, intentional social outreach embedded within its ministries. While fear of the "Social Gospel" in the twentieth century hindered theological articulation of these commitments, concrete engagement that socially and economically empowers the marginalized is a feature of much Pentecostal ministry found around the world

> Early Pentecostalism had a deep, intentional social outreach embedded within its ministries.

today. Satyavrata's own ministry with marginalized communities in Kolkata puts those words into action, with a feeding program providing ten thousand meals a day, clean drinking water filters, basic health care, schools, and vocational training.[2]

Examples like that are repeated around the world. Certainly, there's a diversity of styles and understandings around the relationship of the gospel and social action. As Wonsuk Ma, founder of the Asian Pentecostal Society, explains:

> Too often Pentecostalism is associated with mass media "prosperity preachers" and "health and wealth" ideology. These movements, though not dominant, are persistent. Where they flourish, the gospel is poorer and positive social contributions are few.[3]

Wonsuk Ma has played a key role ecumenically in bringing the stories of Pentecostals engaged in ministries of social transformation to the attention of the wider church.[4]

The term "Pentecostal" is very elastic. Some megachurches in the Global South that utilize Pentecostal gifts and worship style avoid using the name, sensing it might limit their outreach. Further, the lines between being "Pentecostal" and being "evangelical" often seem blurry. But overall, the dramatic shift of world Christianity to the Global South is being accompanied by the rapid growth in forms of Christian practice that place a strong emphasis on religious experience as well as the cohesive value of Christian community.

These expressions of faith are full of spiritual vitality and highly contextualized to local culture. Most important, such emerging Christian movements and their underlying worldview often become differentiated from the outlook of Western culture and the Enlightenment that shaped the character of the Western, colonial missionary effort. That's crucial for those still living comfortably in existing congregations in the West to understand.

Emerging Pentecostalism

Opoku Onyinah, president of the Ghana Pentecostal and Charismatic Council, who also is head of the Church of Pentecost, begun in Ghana and now in eighty-four nations, spoke directly to this question at Empowered21 in Jerusalem. Onyinah led a workshop titled "How Shall We Walk Between Cultures," explaining how African Christianity is interacting with postmodern culture. "It's a new form of Christianity," he explained, "now also living in the West."

Pentecostalism, especially as it is emerging in the non-Western world, is a postmodern faith. I've often said, "An evangelical wants to know what you believe, while a Pentecostal wants to hear your spiritual story." Perhaps it's an oversimplification. But Pentecostalism embodies a strong emphasis on narrative and finds reality in spiritual experiences that defy the logic and rationality of modern Western culture.

Speaking in tongues makes its own sense in a culture where words can't be trusted and where rhetoric is always being deconstructed. Opoku Onyinah stressed why it was important to trust miracles in the postmodern culture. In these settings, "the gospel must be incarnational." People must touch it, taste it, feel it, he explained. That also means an active involvement in arts and culture, the full use of the technologies of social media, and involvement in politics.

Opoku Onyinah is an example of the many Pentecostals from the Global South who have the spiritual self-confidence and integrity to define their Christian faith out of the context of the gospel's interaction with their own cultures and experiences. Such non-Western forms of Christianity are then lived and shared within Western cultures, often propelled by the modern movements of global migration. As a Pentecostal leader and friend from Asia said to me over dinner in Jerusalem, "We don't want to be condescended to anymore."

Understanding Pentecostalism, especially as it is emerging in the Global South as a non-Western religion thriving in a postmodern world, also includes understanding how to grasp the power of its worship and preaching. The connection between the preacher and the listeners is palpable and intimate. Most of the famous Pentecostal preachers I've heard at world conferences would fail a homiletics class at any Reformed seminary. But the purpose is not so much to expound well-reasoned theological truths as it is to incite an intensity of spiritual experience. Such experience grips one's whole being and all the senses; pounding music, singing and shouting, and movement of the whole body, with praying and singing in tongues, creates a synchronized expression of worship and praise.

Niko Njotorahardjo, for instance, is well known in Indonesia and beyond for a healing ministry. More than once when he preached in Jerusalem, he simply broke into song as thousands

joined: "His presence is heaven to me." I've heard Claudio Fre-
idzon, pastor of Iglesia Rey de Reyes in Buenos Aires, Argentina,
simply implore listeners to receive "more, more, more," urging
all to the next step, and next stage, in the filling of the Spirit.
What I've come to understand is that in such settings, those worshipping are longing for, and experiencing, a direct, corporate
participation in the presence of the Holy Spirit resulting in their
spiritual empowerment and giving glory to God.

As Opoku Onyinah indicated, the encounter of non-Western
forms of Pentecostalism within the West is spreading, sometimes in dramatic ways. John Francis, for instance, is founder
and pastor of the Ruach City Church in London—the title from
Hebrew means "Spirit," "Breath" and "Wind." Born in Britain but with Jamaican roots, his congregation, with their slogan
Where Everybody Is Somebody, is one of London's fastest growing, now numbering seven thousand. Those attending are part of
the majority of worshippers in London's churches on any given
Sunday who are nonwhite. The church is present in three different London locations and has started another worshipping
congregation in Philadelphia in the United States. The wider
ministry of Bishop Francis extends internationally.

Kwabena Asamoah-Gyadu, a leading scholar of African
Christianity from Ghana and a valued friend, often points to the
presence of Africans among those gathered at the time of the
first Pentecost. The Pentecostal movement in Africa today, he
argues, is marked by inclusion, promise, and fulfillment. Now it
is reaching those in the West where, he feels, the Bible has been
"domesticated."

Such congregations blossoming in Western societies do feel like a "new form of Christianity." But their roots are in the ancient process of the gospel's fresh interaction with cultures outside of the West, in Africa, Asia, and Latin America. In my view, both evangelicals and historic mainline Protestants in the Global North— people like me—tend to not recognize or to routinely underestimate the ways in which indigenous Pentecostalism in the Global South is freeing Christianity from the heritage of Western, white, colonial baggage, producing forms of faith indigenous and highly contextualized to non-Western cultures. That thesis is one of the conclusions of the *Atlas of Global Christianity*, the most comprehensive academic study of the changes in world Christianity over the past century. Its authors, Todd Johnson and Kenneth Ross, put it this way: "Pentecostalism . . . became the main contributor to the reshaping of Christianity from a predominantly Western to a predominantly non-Western phenomenon in the twentieth century."[5]

> The Pentecostal movement in Africa today is marked by inclusion, promise, and fulfillment.

Such contextualization is always theologically challenging, often messy, but genuinely exciting. Christianity is moving not just geographically but theologically and spiritually out of the comfortable cradle of the Western Enlightenment that has been its home and also the place of its creative and contentious theological journey for the past four hundred years. But now a new agenda is being set. As Christine Caine said in her address, quoting from Isaiah 43, God "is doing a new thing." The question for those in Babylonian captivity at that time and those in captivity to modern Western culture now is whether we will see it.

Part of what keeps us blind is the ongoing institutional isolation of Christian traditions from one another. As mentioned, I attended the Twenty-Third World Pentecostal World Conference in Kuala Lumpur, Malaysia, in August 2013 as part of an ecumenical delegation. It took place at Calvary Church, a Pentecostal megachurch whose pastor, Dr. Prince Guneratnam, serves as the current chairman of the Pentecostal World Fellowship and has been extremely gracious in reaching out to other parts of the global Christian community.

However, the Pentecostal world lives mostly within its own bubble, and those outside of it—both from other Christian communities and the media—remain largely immune from a deeper knowledge and understanding of its dynamics. It's a highly insulated community, normally most comfortable with their own. Historical reasons contribute, beyond doubt. When Pentecostalism first grew, it was ostracized and even theologically persecuted by the wider Christian community. Pentecostals banded together in part for defensive purposes, and often have remained so. This has made several traditional Pentecostal leaders, particularly from the Global North, even more reluctant to engage in ecumenical relationships than some of their evangelical counterparts.

Less than three months after the Pentecostal World Conference, I joined with about three thousand official participants and additional visitors at the World Council of Churches' Tenth Assembly in Busan, Korea. This gathering was more ecumenically expansive, representing the churches that make up the fellowship of the ecumenical movement as well as other guests. Since the Harare Assembly in 1998, the WCC has undertaken important efforts at dialogue with Pentecostals. Yet, given that the Pentecostal movement now represents one-quarter of world Christianity, those are barely first steps toward any meaningful mutual engagement.

Bringing Together Separate Worlds

What struck me was how the gatherings in Kuala Lumpur and Busan represented two very separate worlds. It's as if these two Christian environments have been hermetically sealed off from one another, almost in a state of ecclesiological apartheid. For instance, I'm sure that there were not even fifty people who attended both the Pentecostal World Conference and the WCC Assembly. Having spent time in both of these Christian worlds, they genuinely do feel like two different countries, with their distinct languages, organizational cultures, and values. Visitors between the two often feel like they need a theological visa.

I'm not interested in assigning blame or responsibility for this division. The historical reasons are complex, with divisions in the United States often becoming a major religious export to the rest of the world. But with Pentecostalism's dramatic growth now being driven largely from outside of the West, new opportunities arise for building bridges. In my estimation, this is the most pressing challenge to building unity within the body of Christ in today's world.

Creating such bridges will uncover some unexpected points of connection. One is the link between contemplative prayer and Pentecostalism. On the surface, this seems like perhaps the most unlikely of all connections. Yet, the recovery of the contemplative tradition in the West, interpreted most powerfully in the past fifty years by Thomas Merton, and more recently by writers like Thomas Keating and Richard Rohr, focuses on restoring the primacy of spiritual experience. Rohr calls this an "experiential knowledge of spiritual things," which he argues has been suppressed by appeals to trust in "outer authority," whether imposed by church hierarchy or abstract theological systems.

In this light, Rohr sees an affinity to Pentecostal experience:

Pentecostals and charismatics are a significant modern-era exception to this avoidance of experience; I believe their "baptism in the Spirit" is a true and valid example of initial mystical encounter. The only things they often lack, which keeps them from maturity, are some good theology, developmental psychology, and social concerns to keep their feet in this incarnate world. Without these, their ego-inflating experiences have frequently led to superficial and falsely conservative theology and right-wing politics. . . . But the core value and transformative truth of initial God experience is still there, right beneath the surface, in many people who were "baptized in both fire and Spirit," which is Jesus' baptism (Matthew 3:11b).[6]

Of course, theologians would quickly accuse Richard Rohr of simplistically elevating the role of experience in relationship to Scripture and tradition as the source of authority. Obviously, all of this begs for a deeper theological discussion. But the basic point deserves serious attention. While some may assume that the distance between the solitude and silence of a Trappist monastery with monks in contemplative prayer at 4:00 a.m. and the robust, clamoring, hand-waving worship of Pentecostals with mantra-like shouts of praise could not be further apart, they are united in a deep quest for the experiential knowledge of the living God.[7]

Growing faster than any expression of world Christianity today, Pentecostalism lives in its own messy diversity, often struggling to find its unique voice. But its resolute reliance on the Spirit is its liberating, epistemological pathway. At the same time, the rapid rise of Pentecostal scholarship in theological and biblical study around the world is providing the movement with its own internal capacity for the critical self-reflection that is essential to claiming the distinctive voice and witness that can be offered to the world church. Further, growing opportunities for theological dialogue is one of the hopeful ways that the walls between Pentecostalism and the other parts of global Christian family can begin to break down.

> Growing faster than any expression of world Christianity today, Pentecostalism lives in its own messy diversity, often struggling to find its unique voice.

Pentecostalism and Theology

When Richard Rohr states that Pentecostals lack "good theology," he probably has in mind the suspicion and even disdain often expressed by early modern Pentecostals for academic theology. Such intellectualism in established institutions is what quenched the Spirit, in their view. But all that has changed. Pentecostal theology is now plentiful, creative, rigorous, growing, and global.

My first encounter with the Society for Pentecostal Studies came when I was invited to join a panel on Pentecostals and ecumenism at its 2015 meeting in San Dimas, California. Arriving for an evening keynote address, I listened to Dr. Teresa Berger from Yale Divinity School speak about worship and liturgy. A Catholic from Germany with doctorates in both liturgical studies and Catholic theology, Dr. Berger has been creatively engaged with the charismatic movement within her own tradition. She also has written about the role of gender in liturgical history. Her perceptive address immediately broke down my own stereotypes of what I expected to hear at a theological gathering for Pentecostals.

About 230 Pentecostal scholars from around the world had gathered at this annual meeting. The schedule of workshops and panels covered vast areas of theological, sociological, and historical inquiry. Certainly, it's true that the distance between the pew and the "academy" in Pentecostalism is a formidable problem. But critics of Pentecostalism often fail to recognize the serious theological development that has been emerging in this community, especially in the past three to four decades. For example, I once listened to Pentecostal Bishop Clifton Clark, who has taught in Ghana and now is at Fuller Seminary, present a theological paper about how the African concept of "*Ubuntu*" can contribute to a Pentecostal understanding of Christian-Muslim relations. Put simply, while spiritual experience is the starting point for Pentecostalism, this movement is now demonstrating the capacity to reflect critically on the meaning of that experience and how it informs the continuing theological task.

Pentecostalism's history is also being revised and uncovered by new scholarship. Azusa Street, while pivotal, was not unique. Similar revivals had been breaking out elsewhere, and not only in the United States. Further, the idea that God's Holy Spirit was poured out at Pentecost but then simply turned off for 1,900 years makes no sense to emerging, thoughtful Pentecostal writers and historians. Jeff Oliver, for example, has done a major study, *Progressive Pentecost*, designed for congregations, to demonstrate the presence of the gifts of the Holy Spirit manifested in ways claimed by Pentecostals throughout Christian history.

A Spirit of Openness

All this means that Pentecostalism is becoming prepared to make a theological and ecclesiological contribution to world Christianity that is commensurate to its growing size. A movement that now comprises the largest single group in all of Protestantism and is adding fifty-four thousand adherents a day needs to be taken seriously. But whether the wider church will hear this voice and honor this witness for its own integrity remains unclear. Many non-Pentecostals from mainline traditions need to repent for decades of theological and spiritual condescension. That doesn't remove sharp areas of difference and the essential need for honest and rigorous dialogue on any number of theological, ethical, economic, and political issues. But we need a fresh starting point to recognize and practice the truth that we exist interdependently as members of one body.

As long as Pentecostalism's image in the United States is shaped by glitzy television preachers with private jets preaching a prosperity gospel, it will be difficult to create the mutual encounter with one-quarter of all Christianity that is so needed. Attention must be shifted to other models and leaders that reflect Pentecostalism's emerging impact in the non-Western world. While high-profile, jet-setting Pentecostal preachers are also found there, the reality is far more diverse, often reflecting solidarity with the marginalized.

Take, for example, Marina Silva in Brazil. Growing up in a poor family as a rubber tapper in the Amazon, she became allied with the environmental activism of Chico Mendes until his assassination. Remarkably, she was elected to Brazil's Senate. Having faced repeated cases of malaria and hepatitis, she had a dramatic conversion to Pentecostal faith in 1997. In 2003, she was appointed Brazil's Minister of Environment and won international recognition as a global environmental leader. In 2014, she became the candidate of Brazil's Socialist Party for president. While initially strong in the polls, her candidacy eventually faded.

Silva is a member of the Assemblies of God, the largest Pentecostal denomination in Brazil, which holds the largest number of Pentecostals of any nation. Growing far faster than Catholicism, Pentecostals are drawn largely from poorer and marginalized communities. The political alliances of Brazilian Pentecostals are splintered, with issues such as abortion and gay marriage also playing a role.[8] But a person like Marina Silva serves as an example of an environmental activist and prominent national politician on the political "left" with a strong Pentecostal faith—a combination nearly unthinkable in the United States but completely acceptable in Brazil.

Or consider Frank Chikane from South Africa. Born in Soweto, his father was a pastor in the Apostolic Faith Mission Church, a major Pentecostal denomination. Chikane became involved in the activism of the anti-apartheid struggle and also was trained as a pastor in his denomination. In 1987 he became general secretary of the South African Council of Churches, playing a key role in anti-apartheid efforts. Famously, he took seriously ill during a trip to the United States as the result of a plot by the South African police to poison and kill him.

When Thabo Mbeki succeeded Nelson Mandela as president, Chikane served for ten years as director general in the Office of the President, until 2009. Leaving politics, he returned to pastoral ministry and today is president of the Apostolic Faith Mission Church International. At Empowered21 in Jerusalem, Frank Chikane and I talked about the need for global Pentecostalism to deepen its engagement in broader ecumenical circles, a goal he pursued in South Africa. In a workshop Frank gave in

Jerusalem, he summarized his convictions simply: "When the Spirit comes, people go out."

> When the Spirit comes, people go out.

More recently I was with Chikane again in the fall of 2017 at a conference on global Christianity, hosted by the Myungsung Presbyterian Church, in Korea. Speaking on justice as a concrete expression of love, he said that when we don't see the suffering and inhumanity that God can see, it's because "we have colonized God, and made God into a tribal God." Like Christine Caine, Chikane stresses that the empowerment of the Holy Spirit is given for the sake of missional engagement addressing the pain, hurt, despair, and injustice in the world.

A major test for the future of Pentecostalism is whether its roots among the marginalized and its gift of spiritual empowerment will nurture more than rich personal spiritual fulfillment and be directed toward community and societal transformation.[9] Examples of this abound, but complexities remain in a movement so dependent on the vision of a diversity of charismatic leaders. The struggle for the non-Pentecostal Christian world, particularly in the United States, is to overcome its deep spiritual prejudices and its sense of inherent theological superiority. *Recognizing and affirming the Spirit-filled gifts of the global Pentecostal world and building an open and mutual relationship with Pentecostal communities presents established Christianity in the West with one of its most formidable and crucial challenges for the future.*

Those in local US congregations may wonder where to begin. The answer is likely found at one's doorstep, rather than in funding a mission trip to Botswana. Immigration, the unexpected and largely unrecognized vehicle of God's ongoing mission, is making the realities of the global church local. The growing numbers of immigrant Christians in the United States from Asia, Africa, and Latin America include large numbers of Pentecostals and charismatic believers, reflecting the character of the church in the Global South. The new ecumenical frontier, in many ways, can be found in building bridges close to home that cross the major global divide between Pentecostal and non-Pentecostal worlds.

Those actions, while daunting, will end up being liberating for established mainline and evangelical congregations in the United States. An authentic, mutual relationship will become another avenue for freeing faith from the confines of views rooted in the Western Enlightenment and building bonds with the majority of the Christian world as it emerges in non-Western cultures. In that journey, we will be asked whether we believe the words of Paul in First Corinthians: "we all have been made to drink of the one Spirit" (1 Cor 12:13).

6

■ CHALLENGE SIX ■

Rejecting the Heresy
of Individualism

Of the thirty or so books written by Jean Vanier, *Community and Growth* was the first that came to my attention. At the time in the late 1970s, my wife and I were part of the newly established Sojourners Fellowship, attempting to live a shared life of intentional Christian community near the 14th Street corridor in inner-city Washington, DC. During this period, many experiments in intentional Christian community were springing up throughout the country. They were part of a broad movement seeking to recover the more radical roots of Christian discipleship, with its commitments to solidarity with the poor and life together in community as an antidote to the culture's materialistic individualism.

Building and sustaining intentional Christian community, however, was hard work. Thorny issues of authority and decision-making, the difficult journey of downward mobility, the needs of couples and children, and the ingrained assumptions of personal entitlement all mitigated against the ideal of communal bliss. We regularly turned to historic models, such as the Anabaptist tradition and the Catholic Worker Movement, as well as to persons whose writings or pastoral presence could help on our journey. Jean Vanier's book, new at the time, was an example.

At one point, Vanier explains that for any community to thrive, there must be more members who can say "me for the community" than those who say "the community for me." The truth of that simple insight has been proven in my experience multiple times, in diverse expressions of the church. It reveals the intrinsic challenge of overcoming the sense of individualistic entitlement in any effort to create community. The deeply imbedded sense of individualism, accentuated by the political framework of modern liberalism, corrodes attempts to strengthen bonds of community, whether in church or society.

> The deeply imbedded sense of individualism, accentuated by the political framework of modern liberalism, corrodes attempts to strengthen bonds of community, whether in church or society.

Vanier's words carry the authority of lived experience. A Canadian and Catholic, he is best known for establishing L'Arche, an intentional community of friendship and life together with those with mental disabilities as an alternative to institutionalization. Today there are 147 L'Arche communities in 35 countries, inspired by Vanier's vision and work. He has lectured throughout the world, written extensively, and won the Templeton Prize for Religion in 2015. Vanier's words and life are a clarion witness to the gospel's call to live together in community, voicing a dissonant, countercultural voice to the ascendant individualism of modern Western culture.

Me for Community or Community for Me

That simple contrast—me for the community versus the community for me—captures the heart of the dilemma facing modern Western culture and, by extension, the expressions of the church that are sustained in its midst. As we've already explored, the Enlightenment and the models for political, social, and economic life that it spawned in modern Western culture freed humanity from oppressive, authoritarian rule governing thought, religion, and political structures. The role, rights, and agency of the individual became paramount. This revolutionized the philosophical framework for how society should be governed.

Instead of authority being vested in a monarch with the sanction of God and then imposed on the people, political authority found its starting point with the individual and his (and eventually her) power to give consent to the foundation and functioning of a government on their behalf. This gave rise to the formative idea of a "social contract," put forth by Jean-Jacques Rousseau, John Locke, and others, wherein members of society agreed to certain structures of governance to preserve and secure their rights and livelihood. It was a political expression of "the community for me." In other words, one agrees to the obligations of belonging to a wider community to guarantee and gain certain individual rights and freedoms.

The Declaration of Independence asserts that such rights, endowed by God, are the starting point for government. "All men are created equal, . . . they are endowed by their Creator with certain unalienable rights, that among these are life, liberty, and the pursuit of happiness." Further, if a government abrogates and denies such rights, becoming "destructive of these ends," then the people have the right to alter or abolish it. In effect, they can then establish a new social contract, forming a government that assures and protects their individual rights.

The impact of these ideas in shaping the modern political world has been unparalleled. Colonial rule, despotic regimes, and tyrannical dictatorships have fallen before the power of people and movements that believed that a government's legitimacy is based on the consent of those it governs, securing individual rights. The Universal Declaration of Human Rights, adopted by the United Nations in 1948, was inspired by these same commitments. This radical recognition of the dignity and worth of every individual, supported theologically by the assertion that every person is created "in the image of God," continues to undermine contemporary systems of discrimination and oppression.

Of course, this has not been the only impulse of modern social and political thought. In contrast to individualism, what generally can be termed "collectivism" begins by asserting that realities of social groups are the primary reference point for understanding how societies should be organized and governed. In a nutshell, individuals don't really have a meaningful identity apart from their belonging to a social group. As John Dewey stated, "Society, as a real whole, is the normal order."[1] Participation in a collective group, in this view, is both a more realistic understanding of how society functions and the context that makes individual life possible.

There's a certain amount of common sense to this perspective. Society doesn't function as if it's made up of thousands or millions of isolated Robinson Crusoes. In the famous words of John Donne, "No man is an island, entire unto itself." We live together in essential networks and webs of social cohesion and interaction. For political philosophy, the question becomes where the starting point is: does society find its moral foundation in the rights of its individual members, who then make agreements and social contracts for how best to preserve these rights? Or does society begin by recognizing we are social beings, and collectively we decide—through various political processes—how best to secure

> Society doesn't function as if it's made up of thousands or millions of isolated Robinson Crusoes.

the rights of all who belong to a shared community? Normally this becomes a healthy political dialogue between the primacy of individual freedom and the responsibility of upholding the common good of society.

But ideas can be pushed to extremes, at times with frightful consequences of enormous social evil. That was the case, most dramatically, when collectivism was hijacked by Marxist ideology. Declaring that all supposed individualism was an illusion since the real circumstances and destiny of working people were completely controlled by those who owned the means of production, Marxism proclaimed that liberation would come only through the revolutionary overthrow of the power structure. A new collective state, guided by a vanguard of leadership expressed through a party, would demand complete allegiance to achieve its utopian goals. The results were not only failed economic systems but authoritarian terror, subjecting millions to untold suffering and death.

Individualism has also been pushed to extremes. The familiar term "rugged individualism" was coined by Herbert Hoover in his final campaign speech for president in 1928. The stock market crashed seven months later, plunging the country into the Great Depression. Hoover continued promoting rugged individualism and, apart from major public-works projects, was reluctant to see government intervene in the economic life of the nation, even as social and economic catastrophe escalated. One result was Franklin Roosevelt's landslide election in 1932. More recently, philosophers like Ayn Rand took individualism to such extremes that selfishness became a virtue, dismissing altruism and self-sacrifice and advocating a radical laissez-faire capitalism free of any government interference.

Normally, however, there's at least an aspirational appeal to care about the common good. Think, for instance, of the famous line in President John F. Kennedy's inaugural address: "Ask not what your country can do for you, ask what you can do for your country." It was a political way of saying, me for the community, rather than the community for me. Nevertheless, the dominance of individualism as a primary feature shaping American life is beyond question. For example, the Pew Research Center posed this question to Americans and Europeans: "What's more important in society, that everyone be free to pursue life's goals without interference from the state, or that the state play an active role in society so as to guarantee that nobody is in need?" Fifty-eight percent of Americans cited that an individual's freedom was most important, while majorities in European nations felt the opposite.[2] For most Americans, the starting point is "the community for me."

Life organized around "me" at the center is constantly reinforced. Just look at the apps on your smartphone, which are named "my apps." I have, for instance, "MyAT&T," "MyFiles," "MyChart," even "MySocialSecurity," and my health insurance plan app is "MyPres." My National Car Rental Emerald Club featured an ad campaign based on "The Power of Me." The creative power of advertising in our consumer society, meshed with the tools of social media, wants us to believe that the individual is at the center of everything. All of this fits well with political rhetoric constantly extolling individual rights and freedoms.

In popular American culture, this is the unquestioned starting point, an article of shared social faith.

Biblical Faith and Community

But here's the rub. That assumption is, in fact, foreign to Christian faith. Put simply, it's an unbiblical, alien concept. The biblical story, beginning first with creation, launches into human history with God calling forth a people. Angels visiting Abraham and Sarah promise their offspring will multiply into a people chosen and shaped by God. Moses has the God-given task of liberating a people. They are then led as a community to seek a place, a new land, where their community could blossom together. Prophets call the people of God back to their true identity, forsaking other corporate loyalties.

Then the people, as a community, are sent into exile, where they long as a people to be restored together to their homeland. The promise of salvation coming through the Messiah, the Anointed One, is given to the people of Israel and extended beyond. When Jesus calls people to follow him, he calls them into a community and not to private, individualistic fulfillment. God's presence and power was fully present to Jesus, through the Spirit, as God's only Son. At Pentecost, this same Spirit was poured out to create a new community, the church. This community, together, crosses and reconciles the divisive boundaries in that society—Jew/Greek, slave/free, male/female. All this happens in and through individual identity being placed in belonging to the new community of God's people.

This community is called the "body of Christ." Throughout salvation history, God's action has focused on creating a people faithful to God's love and purposes for the world. Through the life, death, and resurrection of Jesus Christ, people are invited to become members of this community based on God's grace and empowered by the Holy Spirit. Thus, this community, the church, is equipped to embody and carry forth together the presence of Jesus Christ in the world. Just as the Spirit descended uniquely on Jesus as God's Son, that same Spirit now fills the body of Christ, together, in its ongoing witness of God's grace and love.

> Throughout salvation history, God's action has focused on creating a people faithful to God's love and purposes for the world.

Much of the New Testament is devoted to explaining to, exhorting, and instructing those who follow Jesus what it means to live together as a community, experiencing the gifts of the Spirit, and demonstrating the unity and reconciliation that is God's gift. Thus, the metaphor of existing together as one body powerfully highlights the intrinsic interdependence of every member with one another. One's relationship to God is placed in a new relationship of love to one another. This is not an optional choice but a defining connection. Christian faith, incorporating us into the reach of God's grace, binds us to one another as Christ's body.

This Christian understanding of community clarifies that those who follow Jesus are not a random collection of individuals.

Another frequent metaphor for the church in the New Testament is the family. The blood of Christ in this perspective establishes a foundational relationship to others over which we have no choice and that we know will shape the development of our lives. In this sense, the New Testament is full of sociological realism. The life of discipleship, which calls us to follow Jesus's way of self-giving love and to forsake the idols of materialism, pride, and power, can't happen in isolation. It takes a community to shape lives counter to the prevailing values of the culture. Furthermore, it's through the spiritual life and power of such a community that we discover the means for our healing—for both the spiritual trans-formation (*metanoia*) and the transformation of our whole lives.

In this sense, it's true that Christians can say, "the commu-nity for me," meaning that the gifts of God's grace, Christ's for-giveness, and the Spirit's power are mediated through the life of God's people in the church. But far more important, the starting point for one who follows Jesus is always found in God's action to form a faithful people. The goal is to become incorporated into a com-munity that is the vehicle for God's transforming work in the world. The goal is not to find one's indi-vidual happiness and affirm one's individual rights. Therefore, Christians are always beckoned pri-marily to say, "me for the community." That's what it means to be claimed by God and participate in God's ongoing transfor-mation and redemption of the world.

> Christians are always beckoned primarily to say, "me for the community."

Of course, those nurtured in the climate of American Christianity, and particularly its evangelical expressions, will immediately protest. Jesus comes to us as individuals. We are brought into a personal relationship with Christ. All this depends on an individual's choice. Each person is confronted with an invitation to accept the gospel or not. And that takes place in a person's heart, which is then transformed. That's how we become truly happy and fulfilled. Faith is an individual matter, starting there and, finally, ending there. We're saved not by being part of the right group but by being right with God.

There's much truth in that protest. Certainly, our relationship to God is personal and even intimate. Christian contemplatives describe that relationship as one of lovers. Faith does take root in one's heart, and the Christian journey always has an inward as well as an outward direction. But here's the crucial distinction. Christian faith is intended to be personal. Most definitely. But Christian faith is not intended to be individual. There's a difference. We are addressed personally by God. Whether in dramatic stories of conversion or in more gradual experiences of Christian pilgrimage, a Christian comes face to face with God, seen and known in Jesus of Nazareth, who becomes one's resurrected Lord.

However, one's transforming, personal encounter with God's grace and love destroys the illusion of individualism. We no longer live unto ourselves. It's not about me. Our individual self is not the reference point for understanding our role in society and the world. Called and claimed by God's love, we enter indissolubly into the community of God's people. That's where we ground our identity, where we find our nurture, where we experience God's love, and where we discover our calling. It happens together. The great American heresy is to believe that faith begins and ends with the individual, no matter how rugged.

Views of Reality

Where we start makes a difference in how we think. It even impacts how we view reality. Consider this fascinating research done by those at the Cultural Cognition Project at Yale Law School. Scholars wanted to determine why it was that people could look at the same scientific data and reach different conclusions. One pressing example was climate change. Why was it that people formed very different conclusions about the reality and the possible threat of climate change when having access to the same facts and conclusions of nearly unanimous scientific consensus presented to them? It seemed clear that the facts themselves were not determining their convictions.

To find a possible answer, researchers began by looking at basic values and dispositions held by various individuals. Taking a sample of 1,500 people, they determined their underlying "worldviews," placing those on a continuum between hierarchy and egalitarianism and between individualism and communitarianism. Then they asked them to respond to basic statements on certain issues. Regarding climate change, they stated "Global temperatures are increasing" and "Human activity is causing global warming," and asked whether most scientific experts agreed or disagreed with those statements.

The result was revealing. Of those who held egalitarian, communitarian worldviews, 78 percent said most expert scientists agree that global temperatures are rising, and 68 percent said scientists were agreed that human activity was the cause. Of those who were hierarchical individualists, 56 percent believed that most expert scientists are divided on whether global temperatures are rising, and another 25 percent said most scientists disagree. Likewise, 55 percent of those folks believed that scientists are divided about whether humans caused global warming, with 32 percent saying most scientists disagree with that conclusion.[3] The study looked at other issues as well and utilized a variety of means to determine how these various groups viewed issues where there was compelling scientific evidence for specific conclusions.

The authors' hypothesis was supported by the findings of their research. Clear scientific evidence on important social questions was viewed differently depending upon the worldviews or underlying values held by individuals. Specifically, if a person's starting point is the individual, they are much less likely to believe that there are serious threats to our shared global environment. And one who begins believing life is rooted in community is more likely to take responsibility for more than just their own welfare. At one level, there's a certain simplicity to this truth. But the deeper point is that a Christian understanding of our belonging to one another is not just some abstract theological conviction. Rather, it becomes formative, and predictive, of whether and how we live for others, or if we live only for ourselves.

It was Dietrich Bonhoeffer who described Jesus as the "man for others." Those reflections came toward the end of his life, when he was held at Tegel prison and writing to his friend Eberhard Bethge. Bonhoeffer was putting together thoughts for a book never written when the Gestapo cut short his life at age thirty-nine, executing him on April 9, 1945. Bonhoeffer's theological journey, in the face of the rise of the Third Reich, focused on God's transcendent spiritual reality discovered in this world, in the midst of life together, given for others, in the way of Jesus.

Faced with the moral and theological failure of the established church complicit in Hitler's rise to power, Bonhoeffer saw the need for the church to recover the roots and practices of discipleship, in community. He led one of the "underground seminaries" of the Confessing Church in the 1930s, before it was closed by the Nazis. There he established practices to build the life of Christian community through prayer, meditation on Scripture, and identification with the most vulnerable in society. Out of that experience Bonhoeffer wrote his classic, *Life Together*.[4]

As he drew close to his death in 1945, his prose turned to poetry. In "Night Voices," he hears prison guards arriving at a cell nearby to take a fellow prisoner to his death.

> I go with you, Brother, to that place
> and I hear your last word:
> "Brother, when the sunlight I no longer see,
> do live for me!"[5]

For Dietrich Bonhoeffer, following Jesus Christ meant a life lived in solidarity with others, even in death. A life centered around individualistic prerogatives and happiness, upheld by "cheap grace," was a betrayal of discipleship, with both its costs and its joys. Bonhoeffer understood theologically how one's point of orientation as a Christian is to say, "me for the community." Then he had the courage to live that way in perilous times, even to his death.

Life as Relationships

The tension between individualism and community, so persistent within American culture and imprinted on popular theologies of self-improvement, can push us more deeply to understand the nature of reality and life. In 1988, I was called to serve as director of Church and Society for the World Council of Churches, in Geneva, Switzerland. One ongoing project I inherited was exploring the ethical issues raised by genetic engineering. We probed the question of what forms of intervention into the genetic foundations of animal and human life were ethically permissible. Top scientists, ethicists, theologians, and activists were engaged in this dialogue, one that has become even more urgent today.

Dr. Emilio Castro was general secretary of the World Council of Churches and my boss. Without much scientific background on these issues, I was feeling unprepared to deal with the complexity of these questions, so I sat with Dr. Castro to talk this through. He said that the most intriguing and helpful question, in his view, was understanding the nature of life at its most basic level. Did this consist of individual atoms? Or, as scientists were beginning to explain, was the essence of life itself comprised of relationships? And if, in fact, that is the case when examining the most fundamental components of life itself, doesn't that connect to understandings of the Trinity? Doesn't a proper understanding of the Trinity, seen especially from the insights of Orthodox theologians, stress not the three separate "persons" but rather the indispensable relationships of the three together, as one?

It was a conversation I've never forgotten, with its themes echoing and reoccurring frequently in the thirty years since then. The ultimate understanding of reality and the life of the Trinity are connected. Father Richard Rohr is a contemporary theologian and contemplative who has explored this connection with fresh insight, unlocking the mysteries of the Trinity with discerning relevance and meaning. In his recent *Divine Dance: The Trinity and Your Transformation*,[6] Rohr explores how ancient understandings of the Trinity by mystics and early church fathers stressed its intrinsic relational nature as a portal into understanding the essence of reality. He continues to share these themes in his daily meditations, followed online by thousands:

> The Cappadocian Fathers (including Gregory of Nyssa, Basil of Caesarea, and Gregory Nazianzen) of fourth century eastern Turkey finally turned to a word from Greek theater, *perichoresis*—circle dance—to describe the foundational quality of God's character: relationship and communion. In the beginning was relationship.[7]

Rohr continually presses the truth that our understanding of God as Trinity is reflected in God's creation:

Atomic scientists looking through microscopes and astrophysicists looking through telescopes are seeing a similarity of pattern: everything is in relationship with everything else.[8]

This means that community, or communion, is at the heart of all reality. That is God's nature, and that is the core of life itself. Our only place to start, if this is the heart of Trinitarian life, is to say, always, "me for the community." That's not a choice; it's a recognition of our truest identity.

It is against this backdrop that the religious heresy of American individualism, woven into the fabric of a domesticated faith and reinforced by the cultural heritage of the Western Enlightenment, becomes exposed. So ingrained in the heritage and popularized story of our country, individualism has become embedded in versions of American theology that, in fact, are globally exceptional. And that's not a compliment. The expressions are numerous, from the self-improvement theologies of Norman Vincent Peale and Robert H. Schuller to the "prosperity gospel" of Paula White, Creflo Dollar, and Joel Osteen. Faith growing in American soil can readily draw on the culture's taproot of rugged individualism.

The popularity of these ministries is testimony not to their fidelity to the biblical message but to their determination to place the psychological fulfillment and material success of the individual self at the center of the faith experience. In the United

FUTURE FAITH

States, that message sells. Joel Osteen's Lakewood Church in Houston, Texas, is the largest in the United States. In its day, Robert H. Schuller's *Hour of Power* was the most widely viewed religious telecast. And when Creflo Dollar walks his prosperity gospel talk with two Rolls-Royces, a Gulfstream jet, and a collection of ultra-luxury homes, his followers love it, showing the possibilities of God's blessings. The message, it seems, is not just community for me; it's the world for me.

Individualistic self-indulgence will always search for threads of religious justification and blessing, particularly in the crazy patchwork quilt of American Christianity. This tempting message can captivate many. But in the end, simple wisdom prevails as most believers realize that Jesus didn't come to earth to give people Gulfstream jets. Moreover, as parts of society become more secular, those aspiring to wealth realize they don't need a patina of religiosity to make their desires more socially acceptable. Being rich and extravagant carries no social moral judgment, and God really isn't necessary to justify this enterprise.

The Power and Promise of Community

A thirst for community, however, among both rich and poor persistently endures. Expressions of the church that will thrive in the future and that will resonate life reflecting the core of Christian faith will invite people into gracious, accepting communities shaped by the character and presence of God's love. Such communities become the reference point for one's life of discipleship, offering accountability, nurture, and trust. Moreover, they

124

are the social laboratories providing the antidote to the mythical power and attraction of self-centered individualism in the culture.

The biblical and theological critiques of individualism are essential learnings. The discovery of the relational nature of life itself is powerfully instructive. The embrace of the Trinity as a community of self-emptying persons in intrinsic, mutual relationship is an awe-inspiring revelation. But finally, what overcomes the dominance of rugged individualism in anyone's life is the experience of belonging to a life-giving community that tries to live as an embodiment of God's grace and love in the world.

Opportunities are plentiful. In fact, while highly popular preachers espousing various forms of individualistic self-improvement were one stream shaping post-World War II Christianity in America, another was the startling growth of the "small groups" movement. In the 1950s and 1960s, pioneering practitioners of ministry disenchanted with the established church began to discover the power and vitality of connecting disciples of Jesus in small groups of committed sharing and fellowship to empower outward ministry. Often this was described as the "real church" in contrast to sterile and dreary forms of established congregational life.

Lyman Coleman is often cited as one of the originators of this movement. With a background in Navigators and other parachurch ministries, Coleman developed study resources and methods for beginning and nurturing small groups, and it all grew fast. Faith at Work, with leaders like Wally Howard and Bruce Larson, grew as a parachurch ministry stressing relationships and intentional small groups as key to rediscovering the vitality of faith. All this had an antiestablishment, almost "underground" character at the time. At its core, this reflected the desire to recover the centrality of community, or "*koinonia*," at the heart of the experience of living the Christian life.[9]

Church of the Saviour in Washington, DC, experimented with placing small groups, called "mission groups" in their case, at the center of the life of discipleship. These mission groups became the foundation of their model for being the church. This become powerfully formative in my own Christian journey as I became part of this community in 1969, not long after Elizabeth O'Connor had written *Call to Commitment*, the first of many books telling the story of Church of the Saviour. Founded by Gordon and Mary Cosby in 1947, this innovative model believed that combining the inward spiritual journey and the outward call to mission could only be done through small, committed groups. Members covenanted themselves to common disciplines of prayer, journaling, and Bible reading, with accountability, while each group gathered around a specific calling to outward mission. At the time, constructing an alternative model of the church from the foundation of such mission groups was a completely radical idea.

In the decades since Lyman Coleman, Faith at Work, Church of the Saviour, and others pioneering the primacy of community, an entire mini-industry of resources, books, DVDs, Bible study guides, websites, and conferences around small group ministries has emerged. It's almost taken for granted now that a vital congregation is likely to have some version of small fellowship groups. A common criticism is that such small groups can run the risk of turning inward, simply enjoying forms of fellowship, while losing the missional purpose of such groups as originally intended by Lyman Coleman, Church of the Saviour, and others. Nevertheless, the value and practice of community has emerged as part of the mainstream congregational life in countless US churches today in ways that could never have been imagined half a century ago.

In many respects, US congregations now find themselves at a crossroads. Popular streams of spiritually sanctioned individualism, drawn from the culture, reverberate through many parts of the American church. But the communal nature of Christian faith, with its overwhelming biblical roots, has gone from being an antiestablishment practice to becoming almost commonplace. As US Christianity faces its future, increasingly its congregations will need to choose which of these versions of the gospel will claim their allegiance and shape their life and ministry. This is not a matter of accommodating a diversity of views. It's a question of walking faithfully, with others, in response to God's self-giving love.

Here again, US congregations will be helped in their journey of faithfulness by the emerging church in the majority world. The trenchant individualism that has impregnated American versions of the gospel has its roots in modern Western culture. One of the striking differences we see, and have already noted, when Christianity flourishes in non-Western cultures is the altered view of the individual and the community. Here, Christianity takes root in soil that begins, more commonly, with communitarian rather than individualistic assumptions.

Vast generalizations, of course, are dangerous, even if partially illuminating. Yet, I've reflected on this often during my trips to Asia. For instance, the phenomenon of numerous megachurches in South Korea is without parallel. Often, I've wondered how any one of the hundred thousand members of Myungsung Presbyterian Church can feel comfortably at home and not lost in a Christian crowd. On a recent trip there, Deacon Jacob Jung served as my immediate host, picking me up from my hotel each day, driving me to various events, and helping with my local arrangements. Since then he's become my friend. Jung is the CEO of a trading company as well as a deacon, and I learned that he spends about twenty-five to thirty hours a week in various forms of voluntary service at the church. In listening, it became clear that Myungsung Church is like an extended family for him. He belongs, and that is a key part of his identity.

Conversations with many in Korea's megachurches reveal a similar pattern. There's a primary sense of belonging to a broader group that seems natural. And this isn't just abstract. Korea's megachurches are typically organized around small cell groups where such belonging becomes concrete. A sense of identity and loyalty is found through belonging as to a large whole. Students of Korean and other Asian cultures will also point to the strong role of the extended family in these cultures, which provides a powerful social context for one's sense of place and identity. All this begins with belonging.

Of course, there are dangers to this cultural impulse. One need only to look north from Seoul to the fanatical extremes of the forced collectivism of North Korea and the cult of personality around its leader, Kim Jong-un. But I think it's possible to generalize that many Asian cultures begin by recognizing the formative value of belonging to a wider community. When the church takes expression in these cultures, the biblical values of community more easily flourish in ways that are a healthy corrective to the individualism assumed as the highest value in Western culture, and often reflected in its churches.

Starting with Community

Dr. Sam Kobia, the first African general secretary of the World Council of Churches (2004–2009), would often quote a popular African proverb: "If you want to go fast, go alone; if you want to go far, go together." The saying, quoted even by Senator Cory Booker at the 2016 Democratic National Convention, offers a glimpse of how togetherness is valued over individualism in African cultures. When John Mbiti wrote his classic *African Religions and Philosophy*, he studied three hundred different African religions. One of his broad conclusions was that religion in the African context is not individual but always practiced in community. An ordained Anglican priest from Kenya, Mbiti has been a leading thinker in interpreting how the cultural context of Africa interacts with the understanding and practice of Christianity within the continent. The starting point, one could easily say, is "me for the community."

While cultures in this vast continent are extremely diverse, we can focus on some themes in sub-Saharan Africa, where the presence of Christianity is predominant. One is the concept of

"*Ubuntu,*" which has roots in Zimbabwe and South Africa. Its central philosophy, simply stated by historian Michael Onyebu-chi Eze, is that "a person is a person through other people." This means that one can never conceive of their own identity as an isolated individual. Rather, personhood can only emerge out of relationships with others. Our humanity, in fact, is not embedded in our individuality but bestowed upon us by others. That's how linked we are in bonds of communal belonging.[10]

> Personhood can only emerge out of relationships with others.

Bishop Desmond Tutu, the Nobel Prize-winning cleric from South Africa, helped export the concept of *Ubuntu* in his writings. "A person with Ubuntu," wrote Tutu, "is open and available to others, affirming of others . . . knowing that he or she belongs in a greater whole, and is diminished when others are humiliated or diminished." Doc Rivers, former coach of the NBA's Boston Celtics, was so impressed with what he read from Tutu about *Ubuntu* that he shared the philosophy with his team to overcome the individuality of star power so they could play together as one. In 2008 the Celtics broke every team huddle chanting "*Ubuntu*" and went on to win the NBA Championship. The Celtics probably internalized the meaning of belonging to one another in community that year better than most US congregations.

With one out of four Christians in the world now living in Africa, the growth of the church there will be one of the major forces shaping world Christianity's future. This non-Western expression of Christian faith, growing in the communal soil of the continent, connects deeply and naturally with the gospel's premise of our belonging to one another in community. Western individualism is regarded as another colonial import rather than an article of faith. This is another way in which African Christianity offers a needed, corrective gift to US congregations still unable to distinguish between personal faith and individualistic self-satisfaction.

A gospel of individualism fares no better in Latin America. Its long Christian history has been shaped by the colonial legacy of the Roman Catholic Church, although today Pentecostal and evangelical communities are growing far faster and are beginning to change the continent's religious landscape. In the past forty years, the most widely known and exported feature of Latin American Christianity was "liberation theology." Countless books trace its history and debate its legacy. As briefly mentioned in chapter 3, it attempted to reconstruct theology by seeing the world and reading the Bible "through the eyes of the poor." While the way some liberation theologians employed tools of Marxist analysis in understanding societal injustice and power created controversy, the impact of this theological movement in recovering themes of liberating the poor and oppressed at the heart of biblical faith is undeniable.

The method for practicing such liberation theology was found in and inspired by "basic ecclesial communities," also called basic Christian communities. These were groups among the poor who gathered on the margins of the organized church to reflect on Scripture and their own experience, often engaging as well in common work and witness in the face of injustice. Primary was the insight that such expressions of Christian faith could only happen in community. Drawing as well on themes of solidarity within the political currents of the continent, such communities incarnated the conviction that the power of the gospel had to find its starting point in communal life with one another.

While the presence of such base communities may have waned in recent times, that's been offset by the rapid growth in Pentecostal communities. As described in the last chapter, these often find their roots among the poor and the marginalized. This has caused many to comment that while liberation theology stressed the option for the poor, in Latin America the poor are choosing Pentecostal communities. While true, that's also a facile generalization that obscures deeper complexities, which Latin American friends such as Néstor Oscar Míguez have shared with me. Yet the point is that from the range of Catholic to Pentecostal faith in Latin America, life in community is central. Of course, the conflict in the United States between individualistic, prosperity gospel preaching and the gospel's call to mutual belonging in community has been an American religious export, with expressions echoing in Latin America and elsewhere. Yet, the faith of the peoples living south of our border embraces forms and practices of social solidarity that are the normal context for following Jesus.

World Christianity in large measure simply rejects versions of self-centered individualism so commonplace in the United States as the point of orientation for understanding and living out the gospel. The reasons for doing so are biblically, theologically, and spiritually compelling. *The power and promise of grounding faith in community that is so prevalent in global Christianity challenges US congregations to seek a transforming vision of future faith that is not based on the heresy of individualistic Christianity.*

7

De-Americanizing the Gospel

Aiah Foday-Khabenje is general secretary of the Association of Evangelicals in Africa. The organization is comprised of national evangelical associations functioning in forty countries throughout the continent and is completing its new eight-story headquarters, the Africa Evangelical Centre, in Nairobi. Its work is committed to the "total transformation of Africa through evangelization and effective discipleship," and it is one of the globe's seven regional bodies belonging to the World Evangelical Alliance.

A Presbyterian minister originally from Sierra Leonne, Foday-Khabenje travels throughout the continent promoting the work of the association, which serves as an umbrella organization for groups representing about 180 million evangelical Christians in Africa. He also is engaged internationally with other organizations working in cooperative efforts of ministry and Christian unity. For several years, he and I have served together on the steering committee for the Global Christian Forum.

That's what brought us both to Havana, Cuba, in 2017. We were talking together at the Casa Sacerdotal, a charming Catholic guest house not far from Havana's famous Plaza of the Revolution. In our nation's own political revolution, Donald Trump had been elected president of the United States, and he was in the first few tumultuous months of his presidency when Foday-Khabenje and I met in Havana. I had written an article just published for *Sojourners* titled "An Anchor in the Storm" where I tried to state the grave dangers posed by the Trump presidency and then underscore the spiritual disciplines and practices that would be essential to sustain Christian witness in the long term.

Just before leaving home in Santa Fe for Havana, I threw some extra copies of *Sojourners* into my suitcase to share with friends, and I had given one to Foday-Khabenje to read. That's what he wanted to talk about. "Well, I'm glad to know one white evangelical who didn't vote for Donald Trump," he said. Foday-Khabenje was astonished and perplexed at the news of the overwhelming support among white evangelicals for Trump—81 percent of them. They represented views virtually unknown to the community of black evangelical Christians in Africa, as well as those in the wider, vibrant, and growing Christian community in that continent.

My discussion with Aiah Foday-Khabenje in Cuba that day was like countless others I've had since the 2016 election whenever I have left the United States and met with Christians from various parts of the world. While always polite and respectful, Christian leaders from Latin America, Asia, Africa, and Europe shared an incredulity about Trump's election and their grave alarm about the dangers it posed. But most of all, they could not understand the widespread support Trump was reported to have received, especially among white American evangelical Christians.

Even before the election, my global Christian friends were expressing their dismay. In June of 2016, shortly before the Republican National Convention in Cleveland that nominated Donald Trump, I was in Trondheim, Norway, for meetings associated with the Central Committee of the World Council of Churches. Over the endless breakfast buffet at the Scandic Nidelven Hotel and during coffee breaks, much of my conversation was spent reassuring worried ecumenical friends—mostly historic Protestants and Orthodox—that Donald Trump could never be elected president. The numbers just weren't there, I told them, and it was all an embarrassing aberration in US politics.

Nicta Lubaale, general secretary of the Organization of African Instituted Churches, wasn't convinced. We had served together for years as ecumenical colleagues, and the churches in his organization are among the most fascinating in the African continent. All have been started in Africa by Africans, rather than through Western missionary efforts, and often in historic opposition to the colonialism that sheltered foreign missionaries. Lubaale underscored his worry about Trump; he had seen many times in Africa how authoritarian leaders manipulated people's fears and came to power. The church had to be alert to those dangers, even in America, he warned.

In Havana, where Lubaale was also present as a faithful member of the Global Christian Forum committee, we remembered our previous conversation. He was humble, but I told him he had been a prophet, with more insight into the dynamics of the election than most Americans. Like Foday-Khabenje and others, he saw the grave dangers not only of an authoritarian, narcissistic demagogue coming to power but of the complicity and silence of the church in that process. Such sentiments reflect the consensus of Christians around the world. Voices like Aiah Foday-Khabenje and Nicta Lubaale are not those of liberal activists but of well-respected Christian leaders with conservative theologies, known for the testimony of their sincere witness.

Consider this. Originally inspired by the Lausanne Movement, a global evangelical initiative to promote a "holistic" gospel and strengthen missionary outreach, an international group of evangelical theologians formed INFEMIT in 1987—the International Fellowship of Mission as Transformation. They identify themselves as "a Gospel-centered fellowship of mission theologians—practitioners that serve local churches and other Christian communities so we together embody the Kingdom of God."[1] Mostly they are respected evangelical theologians from the Global South.

On January 20, 2017, when Donald Trump was being inaugurated as the forty-fifth president of the United States, evangelical theologians and mission leaders from around the world belonging to INFEMIT released a statement titled, "A Call for

Biblical Faithfulness Amid the New Fascism." It minced no words. While noting troubling trends toward nationalist and racist policies around the world threatening the poor and the marginalized, their call focused particularly on Donald Trump's forthcoming presidency:

> We grieve the part that evangelicals played in electing a person whose character, values, and actions are antithetical to the Gospel. Furthermore, we find it inadmissible that some high profile evangelical leaders have hailed the President-elect as a Christian and a prophet. It does not surprise us that many people, especially from the younger generation, are abandoning the evangelical world altogether.
>
> As representative members of the global evangelical community, we stand with all who oppose violence, racism, misogyny, and religious, sexual and political discrimination by resisting the leadership of a person whose life, deeds and words have normalized and even glorified these postures.[2]

The statement was signed by noted evangelical theologians and mission leaders in Latin America, Asia, Africa, and elsewhere. Certainly, it did not speak for "all" such leaders and made no such claim. If one looks hard enough, one can find a diversity of opinions about Trump in the global Christian community. But listening to evangelical global voices, to say nothing of more historic Protestant and Catholic leaders in the global church, the overwhelming perception was that Donald Trump's election posed dangers that are antithetical to the gospel. More-over, support for Trump among US Christians was seen, gener-ally, as depressing and incomprehensible.

White Christianity in the United States, and particularly its evangelical and Pentecostal expressions, lives in a bubble. It is insulated by a worldview that believes God has a special rela-tionship to the United States that automatically commingles national-istic pride with spiritual righteous-ness. Nostalgia for an "American way of life," rooted in traditional "family values" and implicitly underscored by whiteness, is equated with Christian public vir-tue. Making America "great again," and putting American military power and economic interests "first" in world affairs is accompanied with the assurance of God's special blessing.

> White Christianity in the United States, and particularly its evangelical and Pentecostal expressions, lives in a bubble.

These attitudes are reinforced by the parochial nature of American culture, whose citizens are self-absorbed in expres-sions of news, entertainment, art, and sports that all place US experience at the world's center. Religion is no exception. A self-contained Christian faith living largely in a confined space of nation and race, mostly immune from the influences of world Christianity and racial diversity, seems comfortable and secure enough to endure in this confined isolation. The reality of how Christianity's vitality, growth, and future is being decisively shaped by those living outside of this bubble is neither seen nor imagined.

What amazed so many, including myself, is how politically significant this cohort proved to be in the past presidential election. For decades, important voices had labored hard to wean the evangelical world away from versions of the gospel that were thoroughly captivated and compromised by narrowly nationalistic and racially exclusive attitudes within American culture. A widely heralded watershed moment came when forty prominent evangelicals, young and old, gathered at the YMCA Hotel to draft the Chicago Declaration of Evangelical Social Concern in 1973. Dick Ostling, then religion correspondent for *Time*, said that this was probably the first time in the twentieth century that forty evangelical leaders had spent a weekend together discussing social action.

The Chicago Declaration had a long shelf life in American church history. *Sojourners*, Evangelicals for Social Action, the Evangelical Women's Caucus, and similar initiatives gained prominence in its wake as emerging voices championing the gospel's imperative of social engagement for justice and peace. But by 1979, conservative evangelicals with a right-wing political agenda took up the call to political engagement, with leaders such as Jerry Falwell forming the Moral Majority, James Dobson sharpening a similar political agenda in Focus on the Family, and Pat Robertson building a television broadcasting base supporting the movement.

Beginning in 1980, that movement wedded itself to the Republican Party as an organized voting bloc. Its influence persisted for years until growing numbers of evangelicals began to be weary of marrying the gospel to a narrow, right-wing political agenda. Moderate, mainline evangelicals and institutions kept their distance, and the political impact of this movement seemed to congeal as a predictable but circumscribed portion of the conservative movement in the Republican Party. It continued to exert influence, surfacing every presidential election cycle, but appeared to be losing its organizational political clout. Francis FitzGerald, in her comprehensive history *The Evangelicals: The Struggle to Shape America*, maintains that the religious Right reached is pinnacle in 2005 and then began to wane.[3] The 2006 midterm elections proved disappointing for their fortunes.

On Memorial Day in 2008, I sat at a coffee shop in Chicago with Joshua DuBois, a young African American Pentecostal, before going together to Wrigley Field to see a Cubs game. DuBois had served on Senator Barack Obama's staff and now was coordinating religious outreach for Obama's presidential campaign. Paul Monteiro, DuBois's assistant, joined us. They wanted my advice for a list of diverse Christian leaders Obama could invite to a private conversation where he could share his faith and reflect on how it related to the political life of the nation. My work with Christian Churches Together and the National Council of Churches provided a wide range of potential contacts.

That meeting took place in Chicago a week after Obama clinched the Democratic nomination for president. Later at the 2008 convention in Denver, more panels on religion and faith-related gatherings were held than at the four previous

Democratic conventions combined.[4] Obama's campaign, sensing the discontent of many Christians with the public equating of their faith with the religious Right during the Bush presidency, made intentional outreach to religious voters, including evangelicals, part of their strategy. While the gains were modest, differences in non-Southern swing states such as Michigan, Ohio, Florida, and Indiana were important, and even decisive.[5]

More important, the fracturing of the evangelical world was becoming clear. Earlier, established groups like the National Association of Evangelicals (NAE) had joined a strong coalition pressing for action on climate change. Once Obama became president, the NAE and other evangelical organizations joined Catholics and mainline Protestants in pressing for comprehensive immigration reform. When the Tea Party movement emerged, some in the religious Right made common cause, and polls showed political sympathy toward the movement from grassroots evangelicals. Yet, right-wing politics, in whatever garb, now seemed to capture only a discrete political faction of the evangelical world.

By the 2012 election, the racial divide reflected in the nation's changing demographics was starkly evident in the patterns of voting by religious groups. Mitt Romney won 79 percent of the evangelical vote, and overall white Christians, both Protestant and Catholic, comprised 80 percent of his voters.[6] But Obama's strong majority among Hispanic Catholics as well as his support from evangelical Hispanics and black Christians, combined with other parts of his coalition, overwhelmed Romney's numbers. White Christians, it appeared, could no longer sway an election for Republicans. Those trends seemed to continue. A Pew Research Center survey in 2014 found that only 30 percent of Latino evangelicals identified with or leaned toward the Republican Party; among Catholics Hispanics, the GOP had only 20 percent.[7]

That is why it seemed so startling and even incomprehensible that Donald Trump was elected president and did so with 81 percent of the white evangelical vote. White Catholics also supported Trump with about 60 percent of their vote, and estimates place support from white mainline Protestants at over 50 percent. A key question became whether these white voters were being motivated more by their race than by their religious convictions. While impossible to answer conclusively, since it assumes knowing motives in the hearts of voters, it's also impossible to deny the strong factor that racial fears and anxieties, expressed clearly in Donald Trump's bigoted attitudes toward immigrants, Muslims, and others during the campaign, played in the election's outcome. The clear influence of such racial attitudes was borne out in 2017 as political scientists began pouring over and analyzing election data.[8]

Thus, America's white religious bubble provided crucial support for Donald Trump's surprising election as president. Christians living within this bubble continue to wrap the American flag around their Bibles, frequently obscuring and distorting its words. For instance, when President Trump proposed his suspension of refugee resettlement and a prohibition on immigration from seven (and later six) predominantly Muslim countries, 59 percent of Americans opposed it. Among those in the

United States identifying as "nonreligious," that opposition rose to almost 80 percent. But among white evangelicals, 61 percent supported the travel ban.[9] For them, putting America first meant putting the Bible second.

Some worried that Donald Trump's election portended the new ascendency of the old religious Right. But I have seen nothing of the sort. Certainly, Trump tried, in a clumsy manner, to reach out to evangelical voters. White evangelical support, which was about equal to that received by Mitt Romney in 2012, came not because of faith in Trump's religious convictions or character, which seem nonexistent. Rather, it was motivated by a combination of racial prejudice, economic anxiety, the Supreme Court, and a sense of cultural betrayal by elites who seemed detached from traditional, working-class Americans and their values. Trump captured, expressed, and accentuated those deep discontents, often in ways that were inimical to the gospel in any form.

A Bubble Bursting

Nevertheless, this white religious bubble in America is about to burst. While its impact on the 2016 presidential election seemed shocking, over time it won't hold together as a cohesive force. The irreversible movement of faith across lines of demography, race, and age will undermine this bubble's fragile social membrane.[10]

First, racial changes impacting the church are hardwired into the society, as we saw in chapter 2. Between one-quarter to one-third of evangelicals are people of color, depending upon how definitions are applied. Pentecostal growth is also being driven by nonwhite believers, and the Catholic Church is already a major multicultural body of believers. These trends are accelerating. Despite conservative views on certain social issues held by some of these groups, they overwhelmingly reject the versions of right-wing religious politics, laced with racial bias, that have been encased in the white religious bubble evidenced in the 2016 election.

Second, this white bubble is old. Take one illustrative statistic. Lifeway Research found that among evangelicals who are forty-five or older, 71 percent believe that "God has a special relationship with America." Among all Americans under forty-five, that drops to below 50 percent.[11] Overall, 62 percent of Trump's supporters were over age forty-five, and 87 percent were white. Younger voters preferred Clinton over Trump by a wide margin. Robert P. Jones, the author of *The End of White Christian America*, puts it well when he says:

> White evangelicals in this election aren't value voters. They're nostalgia voters. . . . Trump's line—"let's make America great again"—and his last-minute saying— "look folks, I'm your last chance"—were really powerful for white evangelicals who see their numbers in the general population slipping.[12]

Third, among American evangelicals thought to be the core of Trump's religious support, a fault line within its leadership has been created. Those who aggressively supported Trump, such as Jerry Falwell Jr. and Franklin Graham, often found themselves at odds with other prominent evangelicals such as Russell Moore, Max Lucado, and even the widely popular Bible teacher Beth Moore. Mainstream evangelical leaders and megachurch pastors were publicly silent, keeping a conspicuous distance from Trump loyalists. Moreover, virtually all evangelical leaders of color, joined by several white progressive evangelicals, were outspoken in their forceful opposition.

Most notable was "A Declaration of American Evangelicals Concerning Donald Trump," released in October 2016 by those voices. A withering, comprehensive indictment of how Trump's statements and views were antithetical to Christian faith concluded:

> We have to make it publicly clear that Mr. Trump's racial and religious bigotry and treatment of women is morally unacceptable to us. . . . We, undersigned evangelicals, simply will not tolerate the racial, religious, and gender bigotry that Donald Trump has consistently and deliberately fueled.[13]

An impressive, highly multicultural list of seventy-five noted evangelical leaders signed the statement, inviting others to join. That number soon grew to twenty-five thousand.

After Trump's election as president, polling of attitudes among religious groups continued. When he was inaugurated, a *Washington Post*-ABC News poll found that 66 percent of white evangelicals had a favorable view of Trump. But here's the startling fact: that was the only religious group in America that registered a positive view of Donald Trump at that time.[14] And conservative white evangelicals are a diminishing religious demographic whose glory days are in the rearview mirror as their numbers decline.

Liberating Christian Faith

All this presents US congregations with a pressing challenge for the future: how do we de-Americanize the gospel?

The election of Donald Trump has made it essential for Christian faith in the United States to recover a witness that is not captivated by the polarizing political dynamics of the country and that has the power to convey and model a message that is truly prophetic, biblically rooted, and capable of promoting social transformation. That will require a purposeful distance between the witness of Christian faith and reflexive nationalistic loyalties that verge on idolatry. Faith comes first, not America.

> **Faith comes first, not America.**

In 1971, while working as the legislative assistant to Senator Mark O. Hatfield, an evangelical and leading opponent of the Vietnam War, a newsprint tabloid landed on my desk titled *The Post-American*. It forcefully protested the way Christianity had been captured by the narrow nationalism of American culture, making the church, and especially the evangelical community, complicit in an immoral war and the handmaiden of a system that betrayed biblical faith. Its words resonated deeply with so much I had been feeling:

We find that the American church is in captivity to the values and lifestyle of our culture. Institutional Christianity in America has allowed itself to become a conservative defender of the status quo, a church largely co-opted and conformed to the American system in direct disobedience to Biblical teaching (Romans 12:2). The American captivity of the church has resulted in the disastrous equation of the American way of life with the Christian way of life. This cultural captivity has caused the church to lose its prophetic voice by preaching and exporting a pro-American gospel and a materialistic faith which supports and sanctifies the values of American society, rather than calling them into question. By its implication in the American status quo, by participating in the anti-Christian mindset of our society (racism, materialism, nationalism), the church has lost its ethical authority and has become the chaplain of the American nation, preaching a harmless folk religion of comfort, convenience, and presidential prayer breakfasts.[15]

Those words were penned by a young evangelical seminarian named Jim Wallis. When Mark Hatfield read them, he told me to get this person on the phone right away—he wanted to reach out and thank him and his group for what they were saying. That began my friendship with Wallis, which consistently grew deeper over the decades. This provocative, unknown newsprint magazine struck a theological and political cord. Eventually it evolved into *Sojourners* magazine, and Wallis became a

New York Times best-selling author whose views and influence spread globally and even reached into the White House.

Those first pleas from nearly fifty years ago to de-Americanize the gospel remain timely and have a fresh resonance today. Two things are now different, however, from the tumultuous time of the Vietnam war, the Civil Rights movement, the cultural revolution, and the Watergate felonies of the Nixon administration. First, Nixon's true character and intentions were masked by a slick and talented political operation that was finally unraveled by release of the White House tapes. Billy Graham, for instance, was never critical of President Nixon until those tapes revealed to him a person Graham felt he never knew. By contrast, Donald Trump's narcissistic personality, his vindictive reactions, his nationalistic chauvinism, and his racial bigotry have been on full display for all to see. Christians have no excuse for hesitating to differentiate their faith from those policies and attitudes that are in such stark contradiction to a biblically informed ethic and worldview.

Second, world Christianity has changed radically in the past half century with its geographical center moving away from United States and the West and to the cultures of the Global South. It's imperative that the theological and ethical outlook of US Christians now be re-centered in ways that follow this movement. Our points of reference should no longer be the culturally captive versions of faith bound by narrow nationalism and parochial self-righteousness. Following the global movement of faith means we must de-Americanize the gospel.

Three Steps

Three steps can serve the Christian community in the United States well in this process, which will lead to an enduring and credible future witness. First, we must learn how to listen to those voices speaking to us from the global Christian community and privilege them in our conversations. Second, our priority must be placed on spiritual formation, developing the practices, tools, and communities that nurture faith with roots deep enough to resist the temptations of nationalistic idolatry. Third, our commitment should be to engage society with a compelling public witness, exemplified by actions of solidarity with the most vulnerable, rather than to retreat from society in communities of pious and self-righteous isolation.

Listening to Non-American Voices

One of the most distressing features of American politics is the isolation of conversations. Fueled by the development of cable television and social media, people easily construct silos of political discourse that simply reinforce their existing views. All that has been endlessly documented. But the same behavior inflicts itself on the American church. Christians easily can live in theological and cultural echo chambers that feel safe and become self-justifying.

Yet, listening to a diversity of voices for Christians is not just an exercise of politically correct behavior but a matter of spiritual obedience. As we've seen, the biblical understanding of the body of Christ asserts that relationships between its diverse parts are essential for its health, fruitfulness, discernment, and empowerment. That is particularly true for crossing the divides of race, class, gender, and geography, as underscored consistently in the witness of the New Testament. For American Christians, that is now an imperative for our future witness.

This first strategy, then, is simple. De-Americanizing the gospel requires listening intently to Christian voices that are not simply shaped by the American church. But our unconscious nationalistic self-absorption, often shared across the theological spectrum, makes this far more difficult than we would suppose. Except for Pope Francis, voices of leaders in world Christianity, and particularly from those places where the church is growing the fastest and shaping the future of faith, are typically unheard and largely unknown.

> De-Americanizing the gospel requires listening intently to Christian voices that are not simply shaped by the American church.

That's not because contact between the American church and the global church has been limited. In many ways it's grown, particularly through short-term mission trips, sending groups from US churches to serve on a project for two to three weeks in Latin America, Asia, or Africa, usually coordinated by American mission and parachurch organizations. An estimated twenty-five thousand American Christians participated in such ventures in 1992. Today, it's estimated that at least 1.5 million participate annually, spending $2 billion.

The motive is to serve those less fortunate in the name of Christ. But thoughtful critiques are plentiful, usually focused on whether those dollars could be spent more effectively supporting indigenous efforts of self-empowerment in those locations. Certainly, helping to dig a well in Malawi can be a life-changing experience for a sheltered seventeen-year-old from First Baptist Church in Topeka, Kansas. But it may be that the most important task for American Christians to perform with their brothers and sisters from the Global South is not charitable service but intentional listening. That was summed up by the confessional phrase I saw on the T-shirt of student at a Christian college: "I need Africa more than Africa needs me."

Evangelistic mission and charitable service have framed the paradigms for how the US church—evangelical and mainline—relates to its "overseas" partners. Both function well from the assumption of God's special blessing and relationship to the United States of America. Unless challenged through critical reflection, neither paradigm does much to de-Americanize the gospel. Convinced of our spiritual superiority, it's easier to preach and to serve than to listen. Historically, both our mission and our service have suffered as a result.

It's not that other non-American voices aren't speaking to the witness of Christian faith amid rising chauvinistic nationalisms, a refugee crisis of biblical proportions, glaring global economic inequality, intensifying ethnic and tribal violence, planetary ecological catastrophe, and unrestrained economic greed. Tens of thousands do so all the time. Moreover, such voices constantly warn about the dangers still inflicted on the global witness of

Christianity when the gospel is held captive to versions of American nationalism (whether nativism or exceptionalism), and portrayed as the irrevocable handmaiden of Western culture. It really is a question of who the American church is listening to and what it is hearing.

Leading global voices, which American Christians have rarely, if ever, heard, include Bishop Efraim Tendero, general secretary of the World Evangelical Alliance, which links together about six hundred million evangelicals throughout the world. Its work includes witness and advocacy around refugees, climate change, religious liberty, nuclear weapons, peace and reconciliation, and human trafficking that is grounded in an understanding of faith and discipleship sharply different from the 81 percent of white American evangelicals who voted for Donald Trump. Olav Fykse Tveit is the Norwegian Lutheran pastor who serves as the general secretary of the World Council of Churches. This historic ecumenical fellowship links together 348 member churches (what Protestants call "denominations), representing about 500 million Christians, largely from historic Protestant and Orthodox traditions. Since its last assembly in Busan, Korea, in 2013, Tveit has tirelessly led the WCC on a "pilgrimage of justice and peace," facilitating the churches' witnesses to global challenges.

Each of these global fellowships—evangelical and ecumenical—include powerful voices of preachers, authors, bishops, evangelists, women, youth, church leaders, activists, theologians, and educators from throughout Latin America, Africa, and Asia who forcefully articulate the gospel's witness from a non-American context. On questions such as global economic inequality, climate change, the refugee crisis, and the spiritual bankruptcy of modern, unrestrained capitalistic materialism, their views are in accord with those of Pope Francis. That's because, as explained earlier, he is the first pope in one thousand years to come from the Global South, and his faith and witness bear the marks of one formed in Latin America rather than the United States or Europe.

White American Christians don't have to go to Zambia to listen to the voices of non-Western Christians from the Global South, however. As already outlined, global migration has brought those voices of world Christianity to our doorstep. For many established US congregations, de-Americanizing the gospel can begin with discovering and listening to brothers and sisters who have arrived in our communities and neighborhoods as migrants—and, if we listen, as missionaries to us.

Deepening Faith Formation

The second strategy for de-Americanizing the gospel is to nurture spiritual practices and build communities that shape and form a deeply rooted, biblically informed faith. In doing so, we can learn from important historical precedents. As discussed in the last chapter, when young Dietrich Bonhoeffer witnessed the rise of the Third Reich in Germany, he was dismayed by the accommodation and support it received from the state Lutheran Church and the strong majority of its members. At his underground seminary at Finkenwalde, Bonhoeffer focused on Christian formation, hoping to fashion Christian faith free from its subservience to the nativist German nationalism of the Third Reich. Bonhoeffer understood that the task was to build a fellowship nurtured by a spirituality deep enough to stand the test of that time.

> The second strategy for de-Americanizing the gospel is to nurture spiritual practices and build communities that shape and form a deeply rooted, biblically informed faith.

Gordon Cosby, already mentioned as founder of Church of the Saviour, was also impacted by the events of World War II. As a chaplain in Europe, Gordon came to realize that so many of the men he accompanied lacked a religious faith that was deep and formative enough to prepare them either for how to live or how to die. His vision for Church of the Saviour was for a community grounded in practices of spiritual formation to equip its members for the missional call on their lives. It was not unlike Dietrich Bonhoeffer's attempts at Finkenwalde.

All this should be born in mind when we mediate on the polls of religious voters in the 2016 election. As one who served and led a US denomination for seventeen years, I took this personally. Shortly after the election, I shared this on the *Sojourners* blog:

This election marked the defeat of the public witness of Christians in the parishes and pews of America's churches—and especially those that are predominantly white. . . . That means that those, like myself, who have carried responsibilities to nurture faithful discipleship through Christian institutions, denominational structures, and organizations, have failed in the test of this time.

We find ourselves faced with a challenge like that discerned by Dietrich Bonhoeffer and Gordon Cosby. The public witness of so many who follow Christ lacks the spiritual depth and clarity to proclaim the true meaning of Christian faith for the life of society in this time. Discipleship falters without the strength to follow Jesus into the world. Courage is dissipated, bereft of spiritual power and biblical discernment. The gospel is hopelessly entangled in the habits of American culture and its reflexive, unchallenged nationalism.

Once again, we are in grave need of basic, enduring spiritual formation to acquire both the clarity and strength that equips us to follow Jesus and answer the question posed by Bonhoeffer: "Who is Jesus Christ *for us today*?" The habits of thinking, practices of living, disciplines of praying, celebrations of worship, and clarity of calling can only happen with one another. It takes a community of committed believers to de-Americanize the gospel.

The lesson to be learned is that Christian communities committed to prophetic witness in society endure when they learn to nurture the spiritual depth of practices that equip them for the long run. Resistance alone does not sustain a community. It requires a shared life that is rooted in a depth of spirituality that forms and shapes who we discover ourselves to be and what we are called to do before God. De-Americanizing the gospel in the

Trump era, as in other times, calls us to nurture such communities as integral to our life and witness.

Solidarity Instead of Withdrawal

The final challenge is whether our call to shed the gospel's dangerously infectious American patina and recover its core message beckons us to a strategy of engagement or withdrawal. Pleas to separate Christian allegiance from nationalistic loyalty have numerous historical precedents. Since the Reformation, that path was stressed particularly by the Anabaptist movement—also called the Radical Reformation. Its various branches emphasized the priority of Christian community as an effective counterculture to instill the gospel's values and to follow the plain words of Jesus, not unlike Bonhoeffer's vision at Finkenwalde. For some expressions, however, this has taken the form of a wholesale withdrawal and sharp separation from the cultural and political institutions of society.

Those options have been hotly contested within the Anabaptist tradition to this day. Its most famous recent social and political ethicist, the late John Howard Yoder, argued in his highly influential book *The Politics of Jesus* that Christian witness had to take its roots in the shape and life of Christian communities, but such witness had intrinsic political and social implications, leading to engagement in society rather than withdrawal from it. The early *Post-American* magazine took its name from a biblically radical commitment to free the gospel from its captivity to American nationalism and culture, echoing

Anabaptist commitments like Yoder's as well as the sharp critiques of modern political and technological culture by voices like William Stringfellow and Jacques Ellul. Their intent was always engagement with the world rather than a strategic retreat.

Nevertheless, strategic retreat remains a pathway advocated and practiced by many. That argument has been popularized most recently in *The Benedict Option* by Rod Dreher.[16] Identifying modern liberal secular culture as the greatest enemy of Christian faith, Dreher advocates a strategic withdrawal from many of its institutions and practices. Alternative forms of banding together are compared to Saint Benedict's decision to leave the vice and corruption of Rome in the early sixth century and establish secluded Christian communities, called monasteries, governed by a rule for their life together. Over time these had a renewing social impact on Western civilization.

Much of Dreher's lament about modern Western culture is focused on the impact of the sexual revolution, with its radically changing norms and behaviors and making the desire to be pleased, rather than saved, as a primary goal. *The Benedict Option* is clear about the need to sever Christian faith from its entanglement with national idolatry, and Dreher emphasizes the importance of liturgy and faith formation. But this happens from a strategic posture of cultural disengagement, taking children out of public schools, finding alternative forms of higher education, and nurturing protective communities. Politics focuses heavily on "religious liberty," protecting the prerogatives of such culturally cloistered religious groups.

What's missing is solidarity with those most vulnerable in a political atmosphere driven by nativist, chauvinist nationalism. De-Americanizing the gospel in our time becomes concrete in actions of Christian solidarity and requires a strategy of active engagement in society rather than strategic withdrawal from it. Pope John Paul II said that solidarity "is not a feeling of vague compassion or shallow distress at the misfortunes of so many people, both near and far. On the contrary, it is a firm and persevering determination to commit oneself to the common good; that is to say to the good of all and of each individual, because we are all really responsible for all."[17]

At its heart, solidarity is how we live out the truth of Ephesians 4:25, declaring that we are all "members one of another." It is this mutual belonging to a common humanity that lies at the foundation of Christian social ethics, affirming each one's dignity and building common political and social structures that uphold and protect this commitment. While always a Christian value, solidarity becomes paramount in political climates dominated by division, fueling animosity between differing racial, ethnic, religious, economic, and social groups. Those tensions have infected the climate of American politics shaped by the election of Donald Trump. Language of our common humanity, of our mutual obligations toward one another, and of the need to protect and nurture a political environment protecting the dignity of all is not just absent. Suddenly, it sounds like a foreign tongue.

The vulnerability of three groups requires resolute attention. First, young black men and women are perpetually subject to police actions driven, consciously or unconsciously, more by their race than by their actions. In proclaiming himself as the "law and order" candidate, Donald Trump echoed an old and deliberate message that minorities have historical reasons to fear. His morally inept language of moral equivalence following the white supremacist demonstrations in Charlottesville, Virginia, in 2017 sharply escalated those fears. Christians must be among those who will stand in the gap.[18]

Second, immigrants became a political target from the moment Donald Trump rode down the escalator in Trump Tower to announce his campaign, and they are more vulnerable to capricious actions than any time in recent years. Christians now must take steps to implement the biblical promises toward the stranger, the foreigner, and the sojourner. Solidarity will call us to practical and costly actions.

Third, Muslims have been harshly stigmatized by the Trump administration, which manipulated hostile divisions based on religious differences during the presidential campaign. Those most vulnerable are the 3.3 million Muslims already living in the United States and now subject to judgment, distain, and even violence from fellow Americans. Christians need to build bonds of practical solidarity and hospitality with every Muslim neighbor close to them.

Solidarity requires breaking the bonds of nativist religious nationalism to create the spiritual and practical bonds with those most vulnerable to the politics of exclusion. Such solidarity always extends beyond our shores. A commitment to the common good must embody God's suffering love for the whole world. Pope John Paul II's description of solidarity as meaning "we are all really responsible for all" shreds every attempt to define and confine Christian faith within the boundaries of American nationalism, or any other nationalism. A witness to the gospel by US Christians carrying any global credibility for its future must be severed from its embarrassing and heretical alliance to American pride and power. *De-Americanizing the gospel is now an imperative for churches desiring to announce the good news of the word's presence in the world.*

8

Defeating Divisive Culture Wars

My cousin was gay. Attending her funeral after her untimely death from cancer, family and friends heard inspiring stories of her selfless service to others, her gracious and forgiving spirit, and her devoted love to her lifelong partner and their adopted children. Those three children, now young adults, were born unwanted in other lands and given their life back by Judy and Barb. The service was held at the large Unitarian Church that had become their church home years earlier; it was the congregation that accepted and welcomed them into their fellowship.

This was a long and difficult journey for my cousin. We were part of a strong Norwegian evangelical clan. My grandfather, Carl A. Gundersen, immigrated from Norway as a boy, started a construction company, and became a leading evangelical layman.

He was instrumental in starting Youth for Christ, served as the first treasurer of the National Association of Evangelicals, and was a friend of Billy Graham. All six of his children and several of their spouses attended Wheaton College, the "evangelical Harvard," outside Chicago.

The clan was strong and close, united in part through times spent at my grandparents' summer home in Lake Geneva, Wisconsin. But common evangelical faith was the other bond. On summer evenings at the lake, after playing Scrabble or Rook, we'd listen on occasion to my grandfather recite passages of Scripture. He knew several of Paul's Epistles by heart. While visiting missionaries in Africa with his wife, he discovered a tribal leader named "Big Daddy." Liking that as a nickname, he took it for himself as the beloved patriarch of an extended family shaped by the white American evangelical subculture.

I knew each of my seventeen cousins, staying in touch with several through the years. But with this third generation, journeys differentiated. Some remained closely connected to their evangelical heritage. Others migrated to different Christian traditions, and some ventured onto paths free from organized forms of religion. The broad social and cultural forces shaping the evolution of Christianity and religion in American culture in the last half of the twentieth century were reflected as a microcosm in the journeys of my cousins, and then their children.

For Judy, however, this journey was especially fraught and arduous. Discovering herself to be gay put her on a collision course with all the beliefs, values, and attitudes held by this family's legacy. All this was emerging in the 1980s, before the radical changes in cultural attitudes experienced today. But she was for-bearing, forgiving, courageous, and wise. Trained as a dentist, she used her skills on her own mission trips to Africa, and she nurtured her own loving family, including at their summer cot-tage by a lake.

Relationships with the extended clan were awkward and tense at times, but over the years one reality remained: Judy was part of the family. At her funeral, members of the Gundersen tribe showed up, celebrating her life and giving thanks to God, even in the rationalistic, non-evangelical liturgy of a Unitarian memorial service. Those ties of blood transcended differences of sexuality, ethics, theology, and life experience. Bonds of relation-ship, though tested and at times painfully frayed, proved strong enough in the end to endure.

Would that be so in the church as it deals with the tensions of same-sex relationships.

A Divisive Issue

In the teaching of Jesus, the bonds of fellowship between his followers were even stronger than the ties of family. He turned to his disciples at one point, saying, "Here are my mother and my brothers. Whoever does the will of my Father in heaven is my brother and sister and mother" (Matt 12:49–50). Paul com-pares the relationship of those belonging to the body of Christ to being inextricably bound together as parts of the human body. One part can't function independently of the whole, and each member is linked organically to one another in ways that can't be severed (1 Cor 12:12–27). The blood of Christ binds believers to one another even closer than the blood lines of a natural family.

Yet the church divides, constantly, severing itself from relationships that are confessed to be indivisible. John Calvin described this as "dismembering" the church, cutting it pain-fully into pieces. In our present time, no issue has become more divisive than same-sex relationships and the role of gay and lesbian persons in the life of the church. Media in the United States features headlines that expose the internal strife denominations suffer over opposing attitudes toward same-sex relationships and tell of factions threatening to leave denominational fellowships they long have cherished, and often doing so. Ecclesiastical court cases, with pastors or bishops being tried for taking actions in opposition to denominational policies, or in some cases for simply sharing that they are gay, garner front-page coverage in local newspapers and are broadcast on National Public Radio. Even worse, these arguments degenerate into ugly legal battles around the property, buildings, and resources of congregations that are severed and split over questions of who may love whom.

These ecclesiastical civil wars are not confined to the United States. The Vallée de Joux rests over the Jura Mountains in Switzerland, about an hour's drive from Geneva. It's the region where many of the classic and expensive Swiss watches are made in small local factories by precision workers. Winter brings many from Geneva and Lausanne for cross-country skiing. The area is in the canton of Vaud (cantons are like states in America, comprising the Swiss Confederation). Calvin's Reformation, which was centered in Geneva, continues to leave its mark nearly five hundred years later in the Swiss Reformed Churches in the region.

On a sunny day in May, I enjoyed a leisurely lunch with old ecumenical friends, now retired, by a lake in that valley, and we talked about the life of the local church. Congregations of the Reformed Church in the Vallée de Joux are doing well, and even thriving. Services include families and young people, not just the elderly. The worship style is generally contemporary, with praise songs imported from America that are strong in feeling but thin in content. There's an evangelical flavor to these congregations.

The Swiss Reformed Church is organized by cantons, and the canton of Vaud extends over the Jura Mountains to cities like Versoix, Nyon, and Lausanne along Lake Leman. The Reformed Churches in the canton tried to address the challenge of same-sex relationships, which had arisen in some more urban congregations as a pastoral issue. After much study and reflection, they decided that covenanted relationships of a same-sex couple (not a marriage) could receive a blessing if the couple, the pastor, and the congregation were willing and desiring to do so. If, on the other hand, a pastor and their congregation were opposed to such a practice, they could abide by those convictions. Nothing was imposed—only an option was provided.

The congregations in the Vallée de Joux, however, were aghast. They could never imagine such an action taking place in their congregations and couldn't believe that this could be countenanced by churches anywhere in the canton. They protested, with some threatening to leave the canton of Vaud's Swiss Reformed Church. I asked my friends why these congregations, which had complete freedom to exercise their convictions against blessing any same-sex relationships in their congregations, were so threatened by what a few congregations on the other side of the Jura Mountains might consider doing. There's no clear answer. All this was a familiar story, simply in a different setting.

The irony is that modern secular culture in the West, with the revolution in how information is retrieved and communicated, and how authority is exercised, has spawned growing congregational autonomy, weakening the historic ties within denominational structures. Congregations today no longer look primarily to denominational offices for information, direction, and ministry resources. Denominational mission programs are generally in decline as congregations figure they can make their own mission connections, aided by the plethora of parachurch agencies. Christian education materials produced by denominational offices are a hard sell as congregations feel free to look to many other resources that might meet their specific needs.

Because of growing congregational autonomy, there's increased resentment and even resistance to funds that are required or expected to flow from local churches to "headquarters." Congregational leaders are dubious about the value received, doubting the way that denominational leaders push initiatives that feel like "one size fits all" and ignore the context and unique circumstances shaping a local church. Further, even recognizing vast differences of polity, from systems with bishops to those treasuring Baptist autonomy, congregations want to protect their prerogatives over selecting and providing for their own pastoral leadership. In a word, the trend today is that congregations, rather than denominations, know best.

> In a word, the trend today is that congregations, rather than denominations, know best.

Therefore, it strains all reasonable credulity to hear the protest and threats that those opposed to same-sex marriage voice toward congregations taking a more open approach, especially when nothing compels a congregation to act contrary to its own convictions. Suddenly, denominational ties, which seem to be of such questionable merit, are made so paramount that an act of blessing by one jeopardizes the loyalty of another a hundred or a thousand miles away. The pleas for respecting individual congregational discernment are inexplicably reversed by demands for imposed denominational uniformity on this single question. Such evident hypocrisy reveals the need for uncovering deeper motives and fears involved in the controversy over same-sex relationships.

Global Complexity

A global perspective reveals the even greater complexity and intensity around how the church should regard the love of two people of the same sex for one another. In July of 2017, Leipzig Germany was the site for the World Communion of Reformed Churches' General Council. Occurring once every seven years, the gathering draws about one thousand people from around the world, representing the voices of Reformed, Presbyterian, and United denominations that total about eighty million believers. The priority of pursing God's justice permeated the General Council, and a moving service in Wittenberg, where Luther nailed his Ninety-Five Theses to the church door, proclaimed agreement with the Catholics (and Lutherans) over the doctrine of justification. All now can say that it's God's grace that saves us through faith, and not works.

While this five-hundred-year-old argument between Reformed and Catholic believers was finding theological resolution, pressing conflicts within the communion of Reformed Churches over sexuality were painfully on display in Leipzig. Some of the denominations in the World Communion of Reformed Churches (WCRC), mostly in the Global North, have become welcoming and affirming of those in covenanted same-sex relationships, including giving congregations the option of performing marriages. For others, mostly in the Global South, this is unthinkable. They came prepared to exclude any discussion of the matter.

It's a grave mistake, however, to view this simply as a divide between churches in the Global North and South. While one could hear a preponderance of conviction dividing across these geographical lines, a diversity within each region was also evident. During one presentation, the famous German theologian

Jürgen Moltmann, now ninety-one, gave a moving presentation on the General Council's theme, "Living God, Renew and Transform Us." Three younger women theologians from the Global South were then invited to make responses. And while Moltmann didn't directly address the question of same-sex relationships, Nadia Marais from South Africa did.

A brilliant young theologian now teaching theology at Stellenbosch University near Cape Town, Marais is also ordained in the Dutch Reformed Church. Describing "a church in the spirit of Mary Magdalene," she spoke passionately about how our Reformed understanding of God's saving and liberating grace compels us to accept the gift of those whose sexual orientation differs from the majority:

> It is . . . unthinkable for a church in the spirit of Mary Magdalene to withhold grace from our gay brothers and lesbian sisters, our bisexual friends and transsexual family, our intersex sons and transgender daughters—those who belong with us to the body of Christ . . . not only because it is an injustice, but also because it is a betrayal of the very grace that calls the church together.[1]

Later she told me that many in the church keep wanting to say that faith depends on grace plus something else, like a specific understanding of marriage. Or in the acceptance of apartheid, it was grace plus a specific understanding of race. But it's only grace.

Yet, most voices from churches in the Global South resist even putting the question of same-sex relationships on the agenda for discussion. This was evident, for instance, in Leipzig when a proposal for the WCRC to simply study this question over the next seven years was debated, with vigorous opposition from church leaders in Africa and Asia. This same divide has been on display most publicly in the Anglican communion, with leaders from the southern hemisphere threatening to break their global fellowship over stances taken to affirm same-sex relationships, including the ordination of gay bishops allowed by the Episcopal Church in the United States and others in the Global North.

Understanding the convictions of those opposing such actions is paramount. For those against any recognition or affirmation of same-sex relationships by the church, this is not perceived as an ethical disagreement. Rather, it's a heretical departure from a commitment to biblical authority and a break with historic Christian orthodoxy. They interpret the Bible as teaching an absolute prohibition of any sexual relations with a same-sex partner and stipulating the only acceptable biblical understanding of marriage is a covenanted relationship between a man and a woman. Views to the contrary are regarded not just as differences in ethical teaching but as a departure from revealed truth that threatens the validity of faith and the claim to be a faithful church.

Those views, when held by Christians in the Global South, are often buttressed by a critique of Western culture. A hedonistic lifestyle embracing nonchalant sexual permissiveness, permeating popular culture and saturating the media, is a sinful departure from values that uphold a moral social order. Moreover, when this lifestyle is "exported" to the Global South, it is often described by church leaders as another form of Western colonialism trying to impose a foreign way of life on their cultures. Thus, the controversy over same-sex relationships gets subsumed in the ongoing narrative of the legacy of colonialism, in which the West attempts to impose social and cultural values that are foreign to the traditions of their societies.

Churches in the West that affirm same-sex relationships are perceived by opponents as surrendering to the prevailing moral relativism in their cultures. When Christians from the Global South see empty cathedrals in Europe and declining congregations in the United States, they often interpret this as the result of having betrayed Christian orthodoxy. They are aghast at seeing former church buildings in Europe's inner cities turned into restaurants and even bars. All this fits a picture of declining spiritual vitality in the West.

Of course, these critiques and default lines exist within Western churches, as we have seen. Sometimes walls of division seem ecclesiologically impenetrable. When the Presbyterian Church (USA) allowed local jurisdictions the option of ordaining gay and lesbian persons, some opponents declared outright that the denomination was no longer part of the body of Christ. Blogger John Mark Reynolds wrote, "The PCUSA has removed itself from the line of historic Christian

> Churches in the West that affirm same-sex relationships are perceived by opponents as surrendering to the prevailing moral relativism in their cultures.

churches. . . . Talking to the Presbyterian Church USA will now be interfaith."[2] This kind of demarcation presents the most formidable challenge for the churches' future witness, both within the United States and globally. It takes theological and cultural differences and turns them into religious civil wars.

Conquering the Divide

Defeating these divisive wars in the life of the church is imperative for world Christianity's future vitality. As Jesus put it in the most straightforward way, "If a house is divided against itself, that house will not be able to stand" (Mark 3:25), a quote used by Abraham Lincoln in 1858 in one of his most famous speeches. If Christianity's public profile is dominated by divisive infighting and fracturing over its stance toward two persons of the same gender who love one another, its witness will be crippled. Already today, millions observing the church are unable to reconcile such vicious conflict with the commands of its founder to love one's neighbor as oneself.

Such wars will not be ended in the foreseeable future by agreement on how to regard same-sex relationships. The deep differences present in the church today will endure for some time and will also continue to evolve. Whether in a congregation, a denomination, or a global ecumenical body, the focus must be placed on the nature of this difference and its implications for fellowship. While vigorous dialogue over issues of biblical interpretation, scientific knowledge, theological assumptions, and cultural influences must be fostered courageously, the more immediate questions are these: What is it that makes this difference so threatening? And why should this question determine the boundaries of Christian fellowship?

Answering those questions requires (1) honesty about faith and culture, (2) honesty about the role of politics in the church's discernment of moral issues, and (3) honesty about the diversity of faithful biblical interpretation.

First, culture both shapes patterns of biblical interpretation and is reshaped by the biblical message. It works both ways in a constant dialogue between context and revealed truth. The gospel, embedded through the incarnation, is always heard and seen in highly contextual ways, whether recognized or not. That is the source of the imaginative, missional power of Christian faith, flowing endlessly between diverse languages that are the grammar of cultures.

> Culture both shapes patterns of biblical interpretation and is reshaped by the biblical message.

The last chapter, "De-Americanizing the Gospel," explored the realities and grave dangers that arise when the social understanding of Christian faith is held captive to the framework of nationalistic, American culture. Such cultural captivity of faith requires a courageous interaction between a specific context—American political culture—and enduring truths of the biblical message. Similarly, attitudes in the church toward same-sex relationships are invariably shaped by cultural contexts in any country. Advocates may sincerely believe that they are resting on the "Bible alone," but the Bible is always translated, interpreted, and understood through a particular cultural context. That's true for every Christian.

This doesn't mean that every biblical interpretation is relative. Of course not. But it does mean that every biblical interpretation is contextual. That should be recognized honestly at the beginning of the church's debates about same-sex relationships. Most of my Korean Christian friends, for instance, are strongly opposed to any acceptance of same-sex relationships. They also are shaped by a culture where family honor and fidelity to one's clan is a huge value. Transgressing traditional, familial expectations from one's parents, grandparents, relatives, and even ancestors comes with a formidable cost. That doesn't settle whether the views of my Korean friends are right or wrong, but simply recognizes how those views are held within a cultural context.

The same is true for African church leaders. When they oppose any recognition of same-sex relationships, they are speaking out of a context where presidents such as Uhuru Kenyatta in Kenya, Robert Mugabe in Zimbabwe, Yoweri Museveni in Uganda, former president Yahya Jammeh in Gambia, and former president Goodluck Jonathan in Nigeria, along with others, have not only been outspoken but backed strong anti-gay legislative measures in their countries. President Yahya Jammeh, when in office, called for slitting the throats of gay people. This reflects widespread cultural attitudes condemning same-sex relationships and often calling homosexuality "un-African." Christian voices in Africa both shape and are shaped by this context.

The actual picture of same-sex relationships within African cultures is far more complex, however. A growing body of research and scholarship reveals the practice of same-sex relationships within the wide diversity of subcultures and language groups within the continent. Often not understood in the descriptive terms or binary understandings accepted in the West, the presence and recognition of same-sex relationships within the history of African cultures is clearly demonstrable.[3] Therefore, some contend, with justification, that the criminalization of homosexual activity in various African countries is the actual impact of Western neocolonialism today. Many of the laws on the books in African countries outlawing homosexual activity were the direct result of colonial rule.

Further, it's not coincidental that several of those African church leaders who affirm same-sex relationships, such as Desmond Tutu, are found in South Africa, which has constitutional protections for gay and lesbian persons and is the only country in the continent that has legalized same-sex marriage. Again, this doesn't diminish the courage and integrity of voices like Bishop Tutu's, since the church in South Africa remains divided on this question, but it does point to the importance of one's cultural and political context.

Beyond question, changing cultural values and attitudes in the West also influence the evolution of church leaders and their members who affirm same-sex relationships and marriage for same-gender couples. Presently about two-thirds of all members in historic "mainline" Protestant denominations favor same-sex marriage, a dramatic shift over the past decade. Several denominations, such as the Episcopal Church, the United Church of Christ, the Evangelical Lutheran Church in America, the Presbyterian Church (USA), the Society of Friends, and the Disciples of Christ (Christian Church) either officially sanction same-sex marriage or provide for local congregational autonomy in making those decisions. Congregations in many other denominations also practice full inclusion of LGBTQ persons, including in leadership, which in some cases conflicts with official denominational positions or policies.

This widespread change in policies and practices within parts of US Christianity has certainly been accelerated and supported by changing public opinion. In 2001, 57 percent of American were opposed to same-sex marriage. By 2017, that figure had dropped to 32 percent, with 62 percent in support. Conservative opponents, as mentioned, charge that these churches are simply capitulating to cultural attitudes that are secular and unchristian. Certainly, one can ask why US churches and denominations were not addressing the full inclusion of LGBTQ persons, much less same-sex marriage, twenty or thirty years ago, with a few exceptions. The major change between now and then has been shifting cultural and political attitudes, resulting eventually in marriage equality becoming legal in all states.

However, the relationship of cultural and political values to the churches' positions on moral and ethical matters is far more complex and dialogical. Take slavery, for instance. For centuries, Christianity's social vision accepted slavery, often citing biblical warrant in doing so. The abolitionist movement involved notable Christian voices but also secular ones. At the time of the Civil War, churches and denominations were sharply divided over slavery. Convulsive tensions, conflict, and then war forced

Christians to reconsider biblical interpretations and the gospel's underlying moral imperatives. In retrospect, it would be demeaning to suggest that those Christians who changed their positions to oppose slavery were simply capitulating to shifting political and social views, particularly in the Union. But it's also realistic to understand how evolving cultural attitudes and political movements continually raise questions requiring fresh biblical and ethical discernment on social issues.

> Evolving cultural attitudes and political movements continually raise questions requiring fresh biblical and ethical discernment on social issues.

The plea here is for honesty from all voices in the church about how culture inevitably shapes and influences the convictions that are brought to the controversy over same-sex relationships. Many approach this issue convinced that a plain reading of the Bible is all that is involved or required. But as illustrated, all of us bring assumptions shaped by our cultures, whether recognized or not, that frame our reading and interpretation of the Bible. This doesn't relativize the search for biblical truth; it simply makes it more difficult. Overcoming the divisive, alienating conflict spawned by this difference requires reflective honesty about the constant dance between culture and faith in which we all are participants.

Second, political forces and movements also shape the convictions of Christians—and their intensity—around same-sex relationships. Often, I've wondered how it came to be that relationships between gay and lesbian persons took center stage as the key ethical concern consuming the attention, energy, and focus of much of Christianity in the United States. Other social questions posed serious moral challenges, such as climate change, race relations, mass incarceration, public corruption, immigration, poverty, and many more. But across the denominational and theological spectrum, the stance toward gay and lesbian persons came to transcend nearly every other social question in the last couple of decades. Whether among conservative or progressive groups, it became a priority to address and resolve this single issue, at whatever cost.

Part of the reason was simply politics—specifically, American politics. When the religious Right emerged on the US political scene, traditional "family values" became a rallying cry for support, including opposition in general to affirming the rights of gay and lesbian persons and specifically against any possibility of same-sex marriage being legalized. By 2003 however, it seemed like the religious Right was languishing. The Bush presidency, begun in 2000, had not provided the rewards expected, and the momentum of key organizations seemed waning. In June of that year, a group of key leaders held a meeting in an Arlington, Virginia, condo, just outside DC. Key operatives Paul Weyrich and Don Wildmon called this meeting, and pivotal leaders of the religious Right, including Gary Bauer, James Dobson, and Richard Land, were in attendance.

Several felt that they were losing the culture wars and did not have a clear, uniting message and cause. But one was suggested—opposition to "gay marriage," specifically taking the form of a Federal Marriage Amendment to the US Constitution. That was already in process in response to a Hawaii court ruling allowing the possibility of same-sex marriage. The group decided that defending traditional marriage through such an amendment, as well as efforts in state legislatures to outlaw same-sex marriage, was the political vehicle that could galvanize their base and energize their movement. All this could merge into the 2004 reelection campaign of George W. Bush, pressuring him to be an ally of their efforts in return for their aggressive political support of his campaign.

James Dobson, Gary Bauer, and Tony Perkins, the new president of the Family Research Council, joined with others to focus political organizing efforts around the Federal Marriage Amendment. More joined. Those who met that June became the Arlington Group, whose meetings continued and membership expanded. As the election cycle progressed into 2004, voting one's "values" and defending traditional marriage became a potent political force. It was credited with increasing the turnout and engagement of conservative evangelical voters, which made a critical difference in the close reelection of George W. Bush.[4]

The other consequence of that meeting in Arlington, Virginia, in 2003, probably never envisioned, was to make same-sex marriage, and the status of gay and lesbian persons, a contentious issue throughout the institutions and denominational structures of US Christianity. Once opposition to same-sex marriage became a politically driven moral wedge issue in US politics, the controversy was propelled and heightened in the churches.

Already, the political process had divided conservative evangelicals from mainline Protestants and others in the public square, as political loyalties tended to solidify religious responses. Now this intensified within the church's governing bodies.

Therefore, it was not a process of careful biblical reflection, deep theological study, or discerning cultural analysis that primarily motivated the churches' unending focus on the ethics of same-sex relationships. Instead, this was fueled by those who adopted this as a calculated political strategy in the US electoral process. Of course, various denominations and Christian groups had been dealing with this question, in some cases extensively, prior to 2003. But it was secular politics, rather than detached moral and biblical discernment, that made this a priority issue on both the conservative and progressive side within the churches.

One lamentable result is that the discussion of same-sex relationships in the churches has come with this political freight. It's dealt with as a matter pitting "conservatives" against "liberals," with solutions that can be arrived at only through arguing, lobbying, and voting. A resolution to such conflict is sought through formal actions governed by parliamentary procedures and relying on legal mechanisms such as constitutional amendments. While church groups make good-faith efforts to reframe the climate of consideration with discernment, reflection, listening, and prayer, they are going against the grain. The church's

The church's wells of wisdom have been poisoned by the toxicity of the nation's political culture.

wells of wisdom have been poisoned by the toxicity of the nation's political culture.

Defusing divisive culture wars in the church over same-sex relationships will likely require shedding the secular political models of debate that all bring to this controversy. Any church body taking up the discussion of same-sex relationships must seriously consider how to alter its internal organizational culture and methods of decision-making. Fortunately, models for doing so exist, with a history of exploration and practice.

Discerning Together

Returning to the World Communion of Reformed Churches meeting in Leipzig, an example is found. In its past two General Councils (Accra, Ghana, in 2004 and Grand Rapids, Michigan, in 2010) delegates from around the globe established a process of discernment and consensus in their decision-making, replacing the typical parliamentary-style process. Building on methods originally pioneered by the Uniting Church of Australia and its former president Jill Tabart, issues were framed for discernment and addressed in smaller groups, with shared wisdom then integrated and presented to the whole group (about 250 voting delegates) in a careful search for consensus. This practice takes training, time, and experience, but it leads to results that search for a unifying spirit instead of binary systems of winning and losing.

When the Leipzig meeting took up the contentious issue of whether to study and share in coming years different stances toward same-sex relationships, the process worked its way forward without ever reverting to parliamentary procedure and majority voting. Its decision committed the WCRC, with its 225 denominations, to "set the atmosphere for dialogue and discernment on communion and diversity—in a spirit of consensus building where there are no winners and losers, where no one is excluded, where all are protected and where mutual challenge, mutual accountability, and grace become key values." It's a framework that holds promise for overcoming the typically contentious polarization that seeks to ostracize others from fellowship over the presence and role of gay and lesbian Christians in the church.

The Central Committee of the World Council of Churches, its 150-member governing body, also has been using a style of discernment and consensus for its decision-making for several years. In fact, a growing body of literature and experience has been developing over the past twenty years exploring models for transforming the decision-making style and culture of church bodies.[5] All this is crucial, in my view, for the church's way forward, both in the United States and globally, in dealing with the controversy over same-sex relationships. Transforming the church's discourse, organizational culture, and decision-making style from models shaped by political polarization to methods imbued with spiritual discernment is essential for discovering ways forward. Further, it takes such changes in the culture of decision-making and discernment to create safe spaces for the voices of gay and lesbian persons within those communities to speak and to be heard with open hearts rather than judgmental attitudes.

To summarize, narrow political agendas, not only in the United States but in several countries in Latin America and Africa, as well as polarizing public discourse have inflamed the intensity of the church's debate over same-sex relationships. Shedding the baggage of secular politics is a necessary step in the church's process to have an honest and fruitful conversation and process of discernment.

Third and finally, defeating divisive culture wars in the church over same-sex relationships requires honestly recognizing a diversity of faithful biblical interpretations on these questions. Presently this controversy is often framed as between conservatives who take the Bible seriously and liberals who just ignore the parts of the Bible they don't like, emphasizing instead human experience, science, or other factors. Such a framework is wrong, dishonest, and injurious on many counts.

I'll use my own journey to illustrate. Raised in a strong evangelical home and church in the 1950s and '60s, my automatic stance was to believe that homosexuality was a sin, clearly condemned by the Bible. Over time, learning the personal journeys of gay and lesbian persons, including those in the church, and then sharing the journeys of close family members challenged assumptions I grew up with and had taken for granted. As happens with so many moral and ethical issues, personal narratives created deep questions about unexamined convictions.

When I began serving as general secretary of the Reformed Church in America (RCA) in 1994, the denomination held a conservative, traditional position on gay and lesbian sexual relationships. While proposals for further study were being discussed, the question had not yet become a major polarizing issue threatening division. My goal was to nurture a climate of ongoing dialogue, create space for all voices, and avoid attempts to force a polarizing constitutional resolution.

In the seventeen years of my service, the controversy intensified. We produced study guides, had a three-year moratorium on voting, appointed task forces, endured a painful trial at General Synod, and developed models of congregational dialogue. Very gradually, voices of gay and lesbian persons within the RCA began to be heard. In all those years, I spent countless hours listening to those on all sides of this controversy share from their minds and hearts. In all that time, I never heard anyone say that the biblical witness should simply be ignored or not taken seriously. The same is true in my experience of ecumenical discussions.

What I did hear were clear differences in biblical interpretation. Those opposing same-sex relationships appealed mostly to six specific Scripture verses. Those favoring fully including gay and lesbian persons and blessing their covenanted relationships in the life of the church pointed to limitations in the context of those passages, maintaining that a covenanted relationship of love between two persons of the same gender was not being addressed in any of them. Conservatives pointed to a two-thousand-year tradition of Christian teaching, while progressives responded that other long-established practices, such as slavery and the role of women, have been reversed by ongoing biblical and theological reflection in continuing moral discernment.

In my case, understanding and interpreting the biblical witness and creating the framework for making moral decisions remained crucial. Amongst the growing volume of books and articles exploring these issues, my friend James Brownson's book *Bible, Gender, and Sexuality* proved to be extremely helpful,[6] as it has been to thousands, in exploring the moral logic behind relevant biblical passages and providing an overall framework to enrich our under-standing. Brownson takes the Bible as seriously as anyone and repre-sents fairly the opposing arguments in its interpretation. He concludes that biblical views of marriage in the end have more to do with covenant than with biology. That opens the door to the church's option of celebrating same-sex marriage, which I now fully embrace.

> In my case, understanding and interpreting the biblical witness and creating the framework for making moral decisions remained crucial.

At the same time, I recognize the views of friends, colleagues, and many ecumenical partners throughout the world who hold opposite understandings of how the Bible should be understood and interpreted regarding same-sex relationships. My plea is simple. As with many other moral and ethical issues in the his-tory of the church continuing to this day, we have a diversity of views regarding how Christian faith, informed by the Bible, tradition, and theological reflection, should regard covenanted love between persons of the same gender. The most biblically unfaithful view is to regard these differences as issues defin-ing the legitimacy of another's faith that require divisive breaks in fellowship. Ongoing dialogue in the church's life should be centered in accepting the legitimacy of this diversity of views and recognizing that these views do not question the core of a commonly held faith in Jesus Christ. The truth of the Apostles' Creed and the ancient confessions of Christian faith has never been at stake.

Seeking Common Ground in the Global Church

Overcoming potentially divisive wars within the church over same-sex relationships also requires identifying those areas of common ground even while disagreement and debate continue. Within the global church, it is especially urgent to avoid the simplistic and damaging view that moral relativism has hopelessly compromised the church in the West while the rising church in the Global South carries a unified voice of moral and biblical orthodoxy. Recognizing and protecting the civil and human rights of LGBTQ persons is a place to start, especially since several countries in Africa and elsewhere have highly repressive laws and practices that threaten the welfare and even the lives of gay and lesbian persons.

Within Africa, promising initiatives toward this goal are emerging. In August of 2014, thirty church leaders and scholars from ten African countries gathered at the Thorn Tree Lodge in Pietermaritzburg, South Africa, to discuss how to address the persecution of LGBTQ persons in Africa and change the narrative about how the African church understands these questions. The World Council of Churches also participated. One result was the KwaZulu-Natal Declaration calling for open dialogue in the church's institutions about sexual diversities and condemning violence against sexual minorities. Subsequently, an entire issue of *The Journal of Theology for Southern Africa* on the topic of sexuality in Africa emerged from the consultation.[7]

A second consultation was held in 2016 that included the voices of some African Pentecostals. The Global Faith and Justice Project works to spread awareness of the growing persecution of LGBTQ persons around the world. That task is urgent. Seventy-two countries have laws prohibiting homosexual activities, with a wide variance in how they are enforced. As many as fourteen countries have laws or legal frameworks imposing the death penalty for homosexual practice; in four or five countries, cases have been reported where this has been carried out. Solidarity between churches of different regions, traditions, and convictions in opposing such persecution is essential common ground.

This is made more imperative when recognizing that the recent rise of laws resulting in the persecution of gay and lesbian persons in some African countries with a strong Christian population has been fueled by the direct intervention of those from the religious Right in the United States. For instance, the involvement of anti-LGBTQ activist Scott Lively in Uganda's process of adopting its Anti-Homosexuality Act in 2014 has been well documented.[8] (This Act was overturned later that year on a legal technicality.) Some argue that with the US Supreme Court ruling making marriage equality the law of the land, various activists from the religious Right have concluded that this issue is now lost in the United States. So, they have turned their energy to other countries through campaigns to make homosexual activity illegal. This has amounted to the export of homophobia, and what Kapya Kaoma, an Anglican priest from Zambia involved in the Global Faith and Justice Project, calls the "globalizing of U.S. culture wars."[9]

Defeating these divisive civil wars in the life of the church, locally and globally, requires a firm stance against extremists who advocate the spiritual condemnation of those convinced of God's radical grace toward straight and gay followers of Christ alike, and who advocate the criminalization of LGBTQ persons in their societies. Then we can place the focus on where it must always be: on our mutual belonging with one another in the body of Christ, claimed solely by God's radical grace and knit together through the power of the Holy Spirit. Those ties, akin to and even more powerful than the bonds of loving families, are intended to transcend inevitable differences and endure.

The world will believe that those who follow Jesus have a love so deep that it can only come from God when we defeat angry and divisive culture wars through care-filled listening to and loving one another, showing that we all belong to God.

9

Belonging before Believing

On July 27, 2017, Jeff Bezos, the founder of Amazon, became the richest person in the world. Two decades earlier, he had left a New York hedge fund and begun selling books out of his garage. Now he is worth over $90 billion. Bezos understood that the internet was creating a personalized, direct relationship between individuals and goods they wished to purchase. The person whose fortune Bezos briefly overtook (until a change in stock prices) was Bill Gates, who founded Microsoft, creating the platforms that make information directly and personally accessible to individuals in ways never imagined.

A couple of weeks before Bezos's wealth topped $90 billion, Sears announced it was closing forty-three more of its stores, adding to the 265 already shuttered in 2017. In the past five years, the total of Sears-owned stores, which include Kmarts, has dropped from 2,073 to 1,040. While many complex factors are involved, large retail stores and chains are all experiencing pressure from consumers who are deciding they'd rather shop from their computer while sitting on their couch or while drinking morning coffee in their bed. In 2011 Borders, the chain that had begun in Ann Arbor, Michigan, forty years earlier, closed all its remaining bookstores

My wife, Karin, has contributed to Jeff Bezos's wealth. An Amazon Prime member, she buys everything from cat food to duffle bags online. Last Christmas, the UPS driver who continually delivered Amazon boxes to our house became known as if he were a personal friend. Karin sees no need to wander through a crowded store searching for items and then waiting for someone to charge her credit card when she can do all that from home, and usually for a better price. The only retail outlets she regularly frequents are thrift stores, which have yet to enter the world of online marketing—though some twenty-four-year-old in San Francisco is surely trying to figure that out.

Consider what's happening here. Retail stores build buildings and pay staff to gather, organize, and display goods for consumers to inspect and buy. Encyclopedias collect, organize, and publish volumes of stored information. Libraries collect, organize, and loan books, also serving as centers for research. Taxicab companies organize fleets of cars and drivers from a central headquarters. Hotel chains build, organize, and offer rooms. All these commercial and public institutions, plus more, are being dramatically challenged by how the internet and the technological means to utilize it have radically transformed the individual's relationship to acquiring information, purchasing goods, and accessing services. In 1995, the five firms with the highest value in terms of shares owned were Exxon, AT&T, Coca-Cola, General Electric, and Merck. By 2015, only Exxon remained on that list, now joined by Apple, Google, Microsoft, and Amazon.

On a cloudy, cool day in July, Karin and I landed at the quaint airport in Molde, Norway. We drove three kilometers out of the town center along the shore of the Romsdal Fjord on Julsundvegen, then turned slightly up the hill to a fashionable Norwegian home. Its owners were just leaving, going out to dinner, and showed us into their ground floor, with two bedrooms, a bath, a library/den, and a minimalist kitchen area. It was our home for the next four days. Karin had found the home online at Airbnb. Molde has a sleek, stunning Scandic hotel, designed like a ship's keel pressing out to the fjord. I'd love to stay there some time, but its steep price and small European-style rooms were no match for the value of the Airbnb suite just up the road.

A whole "sharing economy" is developing where individuals can use their cars as taxis with Uber and Lyft, rent rooms of their homes through Airbnb (over four thousand are available in Havana, Cuba), engage someone to do random fix-up tasks through TaskRabbit, or get lunch, dinner, groceries, and office supplies delivered immediately to them by Postmates, to name just a few examples. All these emerging enterprises employ people on their own terms; often they are supplementing the income such people receive from other sources. Many call this the "gig economy."[1]

Several Democratic operatives embrace this as a way to democratize capital and return power to workers. Chris Lehane, a former top advisor to Bill Clinton and Al Gore, now heads global policy and public affairs for Airbnb. David Plouffe, who headed Barack Obama's successful campaign for president in 2008, worked with Uber for a couple of years. As one experienced participant with Airbnb, Caitlin Connors, explained, "Humans can operate on a person-to-person basis, sharing ideas and sharing business without intermediaries."[2]

Removing "intermediaries" like retail stores, hotel chains, and taxicab companies through ubiquitous internet access and ingenious apps characterizes these emerging enterprises, whether they are economic giants like Amazon or innovative delivery services like Postmates. The power of individuals to have boundless, personalized access to information is transforming their relationships to established organizations and structures. Increasingly, people are becoming their own gatekeepers, consuming and working in the economy more and more on their own terms rather than trusting in established institutions to be the mediators of those choices.

> The power of individuals to have boundless, personalized access to information is transforming their relationships to established organizations and structures.

The Effect on the Organized Church

Reflecting on Amazon, Uber, and Airbnb helps illuminate trends that go far beyond economic life. Organized religious structures are also being dramatically altered. The same forces driving Amazon's growth, closing Sears stores, and spawning the gig economy will alter how the church and Christian organizations will function in the future.

Two such trends are reshaping tomorrow's church and being seen already today. First, believers have less trust in and loyalty toward established religious institutions to serve as the intermediaries for how they understand, practice, and grow their faith. They'd rather access information and select resources themselves to support their pilgrimage. They want to choose to join the networks or groups that seem compatible with their beliefs. Second, dogma is less important than community, and relationships often transcend doctrine as a guide when Christians make choices about participation in congregations, groups, and organizations. This feature becomes more pronounced among younger seekers and believers, who begin with the value of belonging.

Most of my vocational life in ministry has been spent trying to nurture and lead established religious institutions. This included serving on the staff and the governing board of the World Council of Churches, and then, as already mentioned, serving for many years as the general secretary of the Reformed Church in America, the oldest Protestant denomination with an ongoing ministry in the United States. I believe in these institutions. They provide a vehicle for congregations and denominations to connect and cooperate with one another in ways that are indispensable. But I also know that such institutions can easily become the religious equivalent of Sears, Roebuck and Co., facing precipitous declines, persistent budget shortfalls, and an inability to maintain the allegiance of many of their participants.

Transforming such institutions is difficult but not impossible. The model for how they function requires fundamental change. Denominational bureaucracies as well as ecumenical and parachurch organizations grew in the post-World War II period by becoming the depositories of resources and initiators of programmatic activities done on behalf of their congregations or participating members. All this implied that a centralized structure had more information and better judgement than its participating members. Thus, a high sense of confidence was essential for members to entrust their dollars to and support distant bureaucracies who "knew best" how to use those resources.

Denominational structures play a further role through enforcing doctrinal standards, rules, and regulations for proper conduct by its congregations and pastors. More practically, those structures typically have provided a means for training and credentialing its clergy as well as administering pension and insurance programs for them. In many respects, denominational structures have taken on the roles of being intermediaries for their congregations and clergy while serving as regulatory bodies. The precondition for these roles is dependable loyalty and confidence from their members.

This model, however, has no more chance of enduring in the long run than Borders bookstores had. A "father knows best" denominational model based primarily on enforcing the boundaries of what clergy and congregations cannot do, and doing things "for" congregations based on assumed knowledge and better judgement, will never be sustainable in an era where access to information and immediate relational connections are on the laptop of every pastor and parishioner. In this new environment, inherited structures of denominations and religious institutions no longer seem to empower their members.

Envisioning New Models

A fresh model would look at how systems like Microsoft provide an infrastructure for the empowerment and connection of its participants. Consider this: A platform allows users to discover with ease the information they need to empower their participation. Software assists in charting the pathways most useful, and then organizing and utilizing the information desired. Moreover, the platform and software become the means for establishing relationships that provide the learning, mutual support, and engagement for carrying out desired ends. The key is that all this empowers the users directly.

Similarly, denominational systems can be reconstructed to focus on empowering congregations, providing pathways for them to acquire needed information, networks of necessary relational support, and expanded opportunities for missional engagement. This requires overturning the traditional model that assumes that congregations have an obligation to empower wider denominational structures. Instead, church-wide structures function primarily to empower congregations in their ministry and mission. Practical systems such as pension programs, insurance, and credentialing can be maintained, but if that is the only "glue" that holds a denominational system together, that system's not worth preserving.

Like operating systems for computers, creative denominational structures will capitalize on their ability to provide strong relational connections throughout their membership. They face a primary challenge to transform themselves, in the experience of their participants, from being primarily a regulatory body to becoming a facilitator of relational networks formed to strengthen common purpose and mission. Examples are beginning to proliferate.

> Creative denominational structures will capitalize on their ability to provide strong relational connections throughout their membership.

The Evangelical Covenant Church pioneered such a model through a midwinter conference that for years has drawn over 90 percent of its pastors to Chicago in the unattractive, freezing temperatures of January. No governance is involved; only relational connection and inspiration. The Presbyterian Church (USA), whose assemblies are notoriously consumed with conflictive governance issues, started its "Big Tent" gatherings, drawing clergy together solely for connection and enrichment. We attempted to do the same in the Reformed Church in America with two "Spring Sabbaths" gatherings for clergy. In that case, we even prohibited any denominational promotional material from being present to emphasize that this event was for our pastors and not another advertising opportunity for the denomination.

The Evangelical Lutheran Church in America launched its first such event successfully in August 2017, held in Atlanta with the theme "On the Way—Together." A few days earlier, Karin and I ran into Rich Mouw, former president of Fuller Theological Seminary, at the United Club in the Denver airport. He had been a speaker at the Christian Reformed Church's "Inspire 2017," described as a "new kind of CRC event" drawing together up to one thousand ministry leaders gathering in Detroit, Michigan. All these examples and more are attempts to shift the energy of denominational gatherings away from a singular focus on systems of governance and toward experiencing the denomination as a place for relational connection, enrichment, and empowerment.

This pattern of empowering ministry leaders through connectional gatherings, however, is also bypassing denominational structures as intermediaries, similar to how Lyft and Uber bypass established taxicab companies. In the evangelical world, the most dramatic example by far is the Willow Creek Association, which has grown out of the ministry of Bill Hybels and Willow Creek Church, a pioneering megachurch in the suburbs of Chicago. Their Global Leadership Summit, held each August at Willow Creek Church and broadcast simultaneously at more than five hundred nationwide locations, reaches over three hundred thousand people. Continuing broadcasts worldwide expand that number throughout 128 countries and in 60 different languages.

The Leadership Network, headquartered in Dallas, Texas, connects key staff and leaders of mostly large, influential churches both in the United States and around the world. Rather than a single large annual event, it sponsors a variety of opportunities linking pastoral leaders and staff together for mutual learning, doing research into trends impacting megachurches, and focusing particularly on patterns of innovation and creative change in congregational life. Its methodology emphasizes peer learning. As an example, it gathered key pastors with technology executives in Silicon Valley to explore patterns of innovative organizational change. Two hundred thousand ministry leaders are served through this network.

"Exponential" gatherings bring together new church start pastors by the thousands in what they call "the largest gatherings of church planting leaders on the planet." Several thousand meet early each year in Orlando, with a program that lists more than 100 speakers and 150 workshops. That's followed throughout the year by similar gatherings in Los Angeles, Chicago, Houston, the Bay Area in California, and Washington, DC. Online training courses, e-books, and other resources are also offered, all in a strategy to support and accelerate the rate of new church starts.

Initiatives like these generally have left denominational activities in the ecclesiological dust. But for some it's not an either/or. Many pastors I've known will enthusiastically take part in a Leadership Summit, join in an Exponential gathering, or participate in other similar events, but remain faithfully involved in their denominational structures, often wanting to import their new learnings into that familiar context. The most influential initiatives, such as those I've mentioned, tend to appeal more to conservative and evangelical leaders, although they try not to do so dogmatically. Progressive pastors in historic Protestant Churches may feel like they have fewer compatible options, although some initiatives like Convergence, animated by author Brian McLaren and others, are growing.

The trend, however, is clear. Whether within denominational structures or beyond, networks of relational connections that empower and equip courageous pastoral and lay leaders serving in environments of continual change will drive the future vitality of congregations. Just as retail stores must creatively incorporate an online presence or else wither and die, denominations and religious institutions must reinvent the models of how they function or gradually constrict into enclaves of survival with decreasing tribes.

> Denominations and religious institutions must reinvent the models of how they function or gradually constrict into enclaves of survival with decreasing tribes.

Of course, the issue is not simply one of functionality and survival. For churches and wider organizational structures, a foundational theological question is raised. Do they exist simply to maintain themselves at all costs, or is their identity defined by uncompromised participation in God's mission? The rationale for reinventing older structures or initiating entirely new networks of relational connections must be rooted in courageous missional faithfulness rather than mere entrepreneurial success.

Complexity on the Global Level

Globally this challenge becomes far more complex. A proliferation of initiatives, movements, alliances, and nongovernmental organizations continue to grow rapidly throughout the fabric of world Christianity. UNICEF tries to keep a list of the religious alliances working just on poverty-related issues; they count thirty such alliances or networks, each of which includes scores, of individual organizations. Then there are global Christian media organizations, countless mission organizations, relief and development groups, global youth organizations, Bible societies, and even Christian trade union and labor organizations. Megachurches have built their own networks of outreach, with extensive mission programs that build hospitals and do humanitarian relief in lands distant from their own.

Added to this is the growing complexity and creativity in efforts of theological education and leadership formation around the world. The rapid growth of the church in the Global South has outstripped institutional capacities for ministerial training and basic faith formation. While seminaries in the United States and Europe struggle to attract enough students to keep their doors open, voices from emerging churches around the world constantly plea for partnerships and fresh models to train pastors, evangelists, and lay leaders for their future. This global misallocation of resources for leadership formation in the church is one of the starkest and gravest examples of internal injustice in world Christianity today.

Jonathan Armstrong, a friend who heads up global theological education initiatives from Moody Bible Institute in Chicago, told me about being in Ghana for the graduation ceremony of 281 pastors who had completed an experimental certificate program. The teaching was done through audio recordings of classes at Moody translated into their local language. Those recordings were then uploaded into solar-powered devices and distributed at no cost to the students. Assessments were done through a phone system. The purpose was to bring theological education to remote locations lacking even electricity and internet access. This is one of many examples of attempts to bridge the gap in global theological training. Frequently such efforts bypass established institutions that seem slow and inflexible in the same way, analogously, that cell phone use is rapidly expanding in Africa, leapfrogging the inflexible technology of land lines.

The continuous eruption of these groups, initiatives, and organizations on the global scene has resulted in a creative chaos in world Christianity. Much of it is driven by the entrepreneurial instincts of US Christian groups. Robert Wuthnow, the noted religious sociologist, documented how the global connections of US churches have grown in recent years.[3] Often this happens through grassroots initiatives such as starting micro-businesses, digging wells, setting up computer networks, and numerous other connections through short-term mission trips. As previously noted, weighing the actual impact of these efforts gets complicated.

Important global organizations and fellowships attempt to provide some coherence to this creative chaos, linking together segments of world Christianity. On three sunny days in May of 2017, the leaders of the most significant organizations—the World Evangelical Alliance, the Pentecostal World Fellowship, the Vatican's Council for Promoting Christian Unity, and the World Council of Churches (WCC), convened by the Global Christian Forum—met together at the Chateau de Bossey, a study center of the WCC outside of Geneva, Switzerland. The gathering made ecumenical history; it was the first time that the leadership of these organizations, which represent all the main branches of world Christianity, had been together for such an encounter.

The Global Christian Forum, the youngest of these ecumenical bodies, is committed to bringing together the leadership from all these branches and expressions of world Christianity. It is the only place where this happens, and three global gatherings have advanced its vision.

In virtually all cases, however, international bodies, including the Christian World Communions (like the Lutheran World Federation, World Communion of Reformed Churches, and a dozen more), struggle to maintain vital participation from their member denominations and churches. And then those denominations are all pressed to deepen the loyalty and trust of their congregations. From the ecclesiological grassroots, these global Christian organizations seem like distant bureaucracies, often with little relevance. The creative chaos of proliferating initiatives, movements, groups, and coalitions often touches the lives of local congregations around the world far more directly.

The organized structures of global Christianity face a fundamental challenge. If they try traditional methods to hold themselves together by appeals to institutional loyalty, from strengthening their apparatus of governance, or through trumpeting distinct doctrinal or confessional identities, they will continue to weaken themselves, with decreasing staffs at year-end struggling to pay the bills while reminiscing about past glory days. These organizations will find a future through empowering their members in common missional engagement and by creating opportunities for building relational connections across divides of region, culture, and theological conviction, which is the greatest strength they offer. That requires creative cooperation with the plethora of emerging grassroots initiatives as well as understanding how a new global, electronically connected environment can be utilized to create virtual communion. As I said to the World Communion of Reformed Churches global gathering in Leipzig, Germany, we need to create "Faithbook."

At the Bossey meeting in May of 2017, I met Bishop Efraim Tendero, the secretary general and CEO of the World Evangelical Alliance. He's from the Philippines, where he previously directed its Council of Evangelical Churches, representing thirty thousand congregations in that country. "Bishop Ef," as he is called, handed me a binder of thirty pages outlining the vision and plans for the "Jesus Global Youth Day" to be held in Manila August 8–11, 2018. It plans to draw together one million youth from around the world for inspiring worship, equipping seminars, and training for youth leaders. Its purpose is to "launch a global discipleship platform to accelerate reaching and building the new generation of Christians."

The organizational effort is an example of trying to collaborate with a variety of networks and groups to mobilize them together toward this goal. In that respect, it models how significant initiatives can emerge in world Christianity's environment of creative chaos. I have no idea whether gathering one million youth for a "Jesus Global Youth Day" in Manila can succeed. Such youth gatherings, however, do happen in the Catholic world. In 2013, their World Youth Day attracted three million to Rio de Janeiro. Another three million pilgrims arrived in Krakow, Poland, for World Youth Day in 2016. The next one is planned for 2019 in Panama City.

Bishop Ef's plans are limited to evangelical and Pentecostal groups, without a broader ecumenical vision. But one could imagine eventually combining the Catholic World Youth Day, an initiative like the Jesus Global Youth Day, and the full involvement of the World Council of Churches in a youth gathering that could dramatically impact the future trajectory of efforts toward Christian unity. Particularly among young people, the doctrinal divides that have kept segments of the church separated in mutual recrimination and distrust have little power to maintain these walls of separation. Differences are respected but not elevated in ways that form exclusive identities or judge others as outside the embrace of God's grace. An interconnected world of mutual belonging has broken down those dogmatic walls.

The Gift of Belonging

On a sunny New Mexican summer day in 2017, Karin and I were invited to the Sunday worship service of Christ Lutheran Church. As part of its commemoration of the five hundredth anniversary of the Reformation that year, the congregation had invited a willing member at each service to share a five- to seven-minute personal statement of their faith journey, under the title of "Here I Stand." On that Sunday, toward the end of the service, a woman I'll call Alysha shared her story.

Alysha was raised in a typical Lutheran Church in the rural Midwest, being baptized there and attending its worship services, Sunday School, and youth activities. Her memories were clear and compelling. First, she found the church services "boring." They held little engaging interest. Second, she found that her questions were not welcomed. She remembered raising issues that she didn't understand and was typically met with responses like "just believe." So, when she became a young adult she left the church, staying away for decades.

Later in life, after undergoing a number of personal crises, she decided to try returning to the church. At Christ Lutheran, she experienced a congregation that welcomed her and her questions. There wasn't the expectation that she, and others, had all the issues of faith figured out. Rather, she was invited to be part of a community where folks accompanied one another in their journeys of faith. This is what drew her in and kept her now as a faithful member of Christ Lutheran Church.

At coffee hour following the service, I sat next to Alysha at a table to talk more. I asked her if the liturgy and weekly communion were something that kept her connected. Not really, she replied. She appreciated it, but it wasn't at the heart of her connection to the congregation. Then what was? The sense of community. She felt a deep sense of belonging and acceptance. She didn't have to have all her questions about doctrine or dogma figured out to be a part of the church community. Alysha could simply rest in her faith in God and in a sense of true fellowship with others. That gift of belonging is what connected her to the congregation.

> That gift of belonging is what connected her to the congregation.

Alysha's story is replicated tens of thousands of times today, throughout the world. Belonging is what connects her and millions of others to local Christian congregations rather than rigid adherence to doctrinal beliefs. Often, the question is which comes first, belonging or belief? The past decade has seen a robust discussion about this, with many asserting that, especially in a postmodern culture, belonging is a step preceding belief in the Christian journey. The traditional view is that a person outside the church undergoes a dramatic conversion experience—he or she reads a tract, or attends an evangelism rally, or has some other personal encounter with God—and then joins a church community. But the more likely pattern in today's culture is that one becomes part of a congregation or fellowship first, working out their journey and defining their beliefs through that process.[4]

Of course, there are still distinctions to be made. A favorite example of how this can function is found at City Church, San Francisco. Started two decades ago as a new church plant in the heart of this city, this congregation intentionally invites interested persons to be welcomed into their life, at whatever point they are in their journey. Their website puts in this way:

City Church is a place for all people, regardless of where you might find yourself on your faith journey. If you are spiritually skeptical, curious about Christianity, or a committed follower of Jesus Christ, we make room for you wherever you are in your process. We aim to be a place that respects what it's like not to believe so that no one has to feel alone and so that anyone who walks through our doors might encounter the work of the living God.

When I've preached and worshipped with City Church, the most remarkable moment for me comes at the "Invitation to the Table" before communion is celebrated, which happens each Sunday. In addition to the traditional invitation, there also is an "Invitation Not to Come to the Table." This is for those who feel they are not at the point in their journey to partake in communion. And they are given a prayer in the printed liturgy for their own nourishment during communion. All this feels very natural and open, without judgment, respecting where people are in their process of belonging and believing.

Those prone to reverse the order of belonging and believing are often impacted by the organizational theory of "bounded sets" and "centered sets." The terms are mathematical ones, but their application comes this way. A bounded set is a group or organization with clearly defined boundaries determining who is in and who is out. Members can be easily classified as being part of this "set" or not. A centered set is a group defined by a clear center that gives it identity, but those belonging may be closer or further from that center. The definition of who belongs to this "set" and who does not is much more fluid and fuzzy. A centered set is more dynamic, and a bounded set is more static.

Paul Hiebert, the late, outstanding missiologist and anthropologist, was the first person to apply this model of bounded versus centered sets to Christian belonging and belief. He did so reflecting on his missionary experience in India, wondering what was necessary for an Indian peasant farmer specifically to believe in order to be part of a Christian community. His articles, originally published in 1978, initiated widespread and ongoing dialogue over applying this understanding to the church.[5] In Hiebert's observations, defining "Christian" in terms of clearly demarcated "bounded sets" didn't do justice to the Christian journey experienced by converts in missionary settings. The direction of one's faith journey was more important, and defining, than intellectual and doctrinal requirements of belief. Thus, Hiebert contended that Indian culture understood the church as a centered set, while Western missionary thinking assumed it was a bounded set.

A metaphor often used to describe the difference between these two ways of understanding the church—and other organizations—comes from Australia. It's said that there are two ways of forming and maintaining a herd of cattle in open land. One is to build a fence around the entire herd. The other way is to dig a well. Whether grazing close or far away, the cattle will always be drawn back toward the water, in a centered set.

Paul Hiebert was a committed evangelical missiologist and anthropologist, teaching at Fuller Theological Seminary's School of World Mission and then for seventeen years at Trinity Evangelical Divinity School, leading its missiological and intercultural studies program. His thinking about how to understand the church, as well as the issues of contextualization in mission, have had widespread influence throughout the Christian community. In my view, these perspectives are pivotal in grasping the nature of changes in the organizational and institutional dynamics of world Christianity.

Alysha was really looking for, and discovering, a Christian community that functioned as a centered set. That doesn't mean there's an absence of doctrine or theological conviction. Congregations like hers will regularly recite the Apostles' Creed. But the animating force in such congregations is relational connection. This trend becomes more pronounced when the church moves out of the mind-set and matrix of Western culture. Hiebert's observation forty years ago about the different understandings of the church between Indian and Western mind-sets describes a major movement in the global church today as Christianity emerges predominantly as a non-Western religion.

All of this impacts local congregations in the United States and the Western world. Across the theological spectrum, we've inherited understandings of the church that are framed, consciously or unconsciously, as bounded sets. Belonging is a derivative of belief. But that paradigm is undergoing a fundamental change. Adapting to this change will become critical to future congregational vitality. Evangelical pastor John Ortberg, formerly at Willow Creek Church, explains what it means to focus on Jesus and understand the church as a centered set:

> We realize that God is in a much better position than we are to know who's in and who's out. We also realize that everyone has something to learn, that everyone has a next step to take, and we don't have to make ourselves seem more different than we really are. We embrace our common humanity.[6]

In such a changed paradigm, doctrine becomes the servant of the community rather than its master.

In summary, technological, economic, and social innovations sweeping the globe are producing two irreversible changes throughout world Christianity. First, adherents of faith have less trust and loyalty toward established religious institutions, especially as they attempt to determine for their followers patterns of belief and religious practices to guide their daily lives. Second, participation in local Christian congregations and groups is being driven more by the experience of belonging to a welcoming, nurturing community than by doctrinal agreement and dogmatic belief.

Discerning and honest global Christian leaders sense that present structures and paradigms are faltering and appear to be incapable of supporting future faith. Evangelicals have anxiety over how to maintain doctrinal purity in the face of perceived relational relativism. Historic Protestants ponder the fate of diminishing congregations and weakening denominational structures all built as bounded sets that assume loyal membership. Catholic officialdom worries about how any sense of centralized authority can be freely maintained in the face of historically unprecedented developments radically decentralizing access to information and the exercise of power.

But the irony is that Christian faith continues to expand and grow globally. It no longer is conforming to the old and worn wineskins of Western culture and organizational structures. *Participation in communities nurturing future faith will be driven by relational connections rather than defined by doctrinal divides.* The church that will learn to survive and thrive in this future will be one that includes rather than excludes, that welcomes rather than warns, and that relates rather than regulates.

10

Saving *This* World

Doug Leonard and I sat together on the patio of my home in Santa Fe on a beautiful September day. He had flown to see me, and at the time he was serving as director of Global Mission for the Reformed Church in America. Now he's the World Council of Churches' representative to the United Nations. His passion and spiritual excitement became evident when he began sharing the story of a recent trip to the Omo Valley in Ethiopia.

About twenty years ago, a missionary couple was sent to minister amongst a tribal group that herded cattle and depended on sorghum as feed. Sustainable irrigation was needed, however, and the missionaries trained those in the tribe to build, install, and maintain simple windmills to pump water to the fields, especially essential in times of drought. Otherwise crops fail, cattle can't feed, food becomes scarce, and children are threatened with starvation. During a seven-year drought, it was estimated that this irrigation system carefully utilizing available water probably saved more than five thousand children.

Bible studies were begun. Over a long time, a church community of 150 tribal members emerged, with fully indigenous leaders, hymns, and worship style. They began training and sending those leaders as "missionaries" to other areas. The tribe had regularly engaged in conflict with other tribes in old patterns, stealing cattle and sometimes killing rivals, especially as AK-47s became available. But church leaders determined that those actions were against Christ's love and had to stop. Similarly, patterns of wife beating with special whips were part of the culture, but church members ceased the practice, changing husband-wife relationships.

Leonard concluded, "The gospel cannot be separated from works of compassion and justice. And works of compassion and justice lack sustainability, local buy-in, and life when they are separated from the gospel. . . . [W]hen hearts are brought into contact with the living, exhilarating, life-giving, shame-erasing love of Christ, profound reform takes place within the lives of people and within the practices of their society."

Works of compassion and justice lack sustainability, local buy-in, and life when they are separated from the gospel.

This inspiring story is one of tens of thousands that come from the emerging church in the Global South. Its salient features are these:

1. When Christian faith is introduced into a new culture, this happens in a specific economic, social, and political context. If this faith doesn't make a practical difference for good in the daily life of people—in this case through irrigating crops—its relevance will be doubted.

2. The gospel has a personal, transforming impact in the lives of those who decide to follow Jesus. People's behaviors within their specific cultural context begin to change, also creating a dialogue between gospel and culture.

3. The community—an indigenous congregation, prayer group, or action/reflection group—becomes an indispensable body that shapes and reinforces changed behavior. Belonging to a Christian community seems intrinsic, not optional, and such communities become the agents of wider cultural change.

A Damaging Divide

This, of course, is not the way Christian faith in the West has been typically understood and practiced, especially in the last century. The most damaging blow to Christian witness in the twentieth century was the sharp division between what came to be known as evangelicalism (originally fundamentalism) and the social gospel. Its history has been recounted many times, but its legacy persists, in part because this division became institutionalized. We know the story, and many of those reading these words have been its subjects as well as its victims.

Suffice it to say that in the early twentieth century, a major theological conflict ensued in the United States, beginning in the Presbyterian Church. A group insisting on upholding the "fundamentals" of faith, such as inerrancy and a literal interpretation of the Bible as well as the virgin birth, protested "modernist" trends they saw advocated by those in denominational and theological leadership, including Princeton Seminary. The fight that ensued was prolonged and often rhetorically vicious, spreading to virtually every denomination in the United States.

The most historically famous incident was the Scopes Trial, in which the teaching of evolution as espoused by Charles Darwin was debated. Clarence Darrow was pitted against William Jennings Bryan, and the event became a media circus, with the perception that Bryan and the fundamentalists had lost the public argument. But this was only the tip of an ecclesiastical iceberg of controversy that raged through the 1920s and beyond over the control of theological seminaries, denominations, and other church institutions. The "modernists" generally won the day in terms of maintaining their power in traditional church institutions.

The fundamentalist public retreat, however, proved to be anything but a defeat. They went on to form and support a whole alternative set of institutions, including colleges, seminaries, denominations, and parachurch organizations. Ecumenism also become embroiled in this controversy. Early explorations, such as the Federal Council of Churches, were led by those in the modernist camp. After World War II, when the World Council of Churches and National Council of Churches (USA) were founded, the fundamentalist groups put in place the World Evangelical Fellowship and the National Association of Evangelicals as alternatives.

Leaders inheriting the fundamentalist tradition tried to soften its sharp edges and engage culture more creatively, adopting the "evangelical" label and founding institutions such as Fuller Seminary and parachurch organizations such as Youth for Christ, Young Life, InterVarsity, World Vision, and many more. But by the middle of the twentieth century, the lines of theological division instigated by the fundamentalist-modernist controversy in the 1920s had become institutionalized. Protestant Christians found themselves living largely in two different ecclesiastical worlds, with separate congregations, denominations, interchurch organizations, and theological institutions.

The evangelical world stressed the essential need of an individual's personal encounter of faith in Jesus Christ as Lord and Savior. With this went a conservative theological view of major doctrines and inerrant understandings of biblical authority. This was accompanied by a view of politics stressing individual responsibility and personal morality that tilted toward the political Right; later that tendency was exploited by conservative Republican politicians, as discussed in chapter 7.

The mainline Protestant or "liberal" world stressed the biblical call to social justice as primary to its witness. Inheriting forms of the "social gospel" movement, it was less rigid on doctrinal orthodoxy and open to involvement in the Civil Rights movement and similar social issues. While not doctrinaire, this tilted toward more Democratic political directions, supporting the tradition of progressive social change.

This general historical summary, frequently set forth in popularized church history, omits certain parts of the non-Catholic world in the United States. Most notably, the historic black churches are absent, whose long presence has carried a witness that is both evangelical and committed to social justice. Further, the Orthodox churches in the United States are omitted. They don't fit this simple dichotomy, since they are ecumenically committed but are also defenders of the historic tradition of Christian faith. Moreover, Pentecostalism, while included organizationally in groups such as the National Association of Evangelicals, was marginalized until its more recent growth accentuated its distinct identity. Even with these caveats, however, this rigid dichotomy between fundamentalists and modernists, which morphed into an institutionalized division between evangelicals and liberals, defined non-Catholic faith in the United States.

This tragedy was compounded as these polarized, competing versions of Christian faith became the primary theological export of the United States around the world. This was reflected in the modern missionary movement as well as in the intentional competition between evangelical global organizations and ecumenical ones. The rise of global communications and religious broadcasting tended to drive this theological wedge further within world Christianity.

However, the massive movement of the Christian community to the Global South is overcoming this dichotomous faith exported from the United States. This is happening simply because the majority of lived Christian experience in the world is now grounded in a different context. Chapter 7 emphasized the importance of listening to the fresh voices emerging from this new Christian majority in order to "de-Americanize" the gospel.

What we hear, increasingly, is the rejection of the impulse to conceive of Christian faith as a binary choice between personal conversion and social justice. Further, we witness an unwillingness to divide the world Christian community into competing camps based on such an erroneous understanding of faith.

> What we hear, increasingly, is the rejection of the impulse to conceive of Christian faith as a binary choice between personal conversion and social justice.

When I served with the World Council of Churches (WCC) in the early 1990s, one of my projects was to arrange a dialogue meeting between the leaders of World Vision International and the WCC. At the time, this was no easy task, requiring persistent ecumenical diplomacy. Some in the WCC considered World Vision as a chief competitor, with a shallow, paternalistic theology and conservative funding that eroded ecumenical commitments. International leaders of World Vision were concerned that some supporters would learn of their presence in the WCC's ecumenical center in Geneva, which many of their US backers regarded as a source of liberal heresy.

But when we finally convened the meeting, we invited those who were partners of World Vision and of the WCC rooted in the Global South, and particularly Africa, to be part of this dialogue. That proved revealing. After listening to the differing narratives of World Vision and the WCC, one of the Africans finally said, "In our part of the world, we have a saying: 'When two elephants fight, our grass gets trampled.'" His meaning could not have been clearer. The perceived conflict between "liberal" and "evangelical" institutions was a product of the Global North. It was not only irrelevant to his region, it also did damage.

Signs of Hope

In my own ecumenical experience, it's hard to name a single African Christian I've known who would not offer a warm testimony to his or her personal faith in Jesus Christ. And I cannot imagine any one of them not feeling passionate, as a follower of Jesus, about the issues of poverty, HIV/AIDS, corruption, human rights, and global economic injustice. Further, they nearly always root those experiences in a local congregation or Christian community that plays a central role in their lives. And by 2025, 40 percent of all Christians worldwide will be living out their faith in Africa.

Similar observations could be offered about Pentecostals building new Christian communities among the poor and marginalized in the barrios of Sao Paulo, Brazil. In India the Evangelical Social Action Forum, launched in the state of Kerala, is committed to the "sustainable wholistic transformation of the poor and the marginalized for a just and fair society." It's one of hundreds of community development organizations that have emerged from evangelical networks in the Global South over the past three decades. Most are linked in the Micah Network, founded in 1999, now numbering over six hundred organizations in eighty-six countries.

The Micah Network is a "Global Partner" of the World Evangelical Alliance but also works with a variety of ecumenical networks in its advocacy efforts. It focuses on "integral mission," which is defined this way:

> If we ignore the world we betray the word of God, which sends us out to serve the world. If we ignore the word of God we have nothing to bring to the world. Justice and justification by faith, worship and political action, the spiritual and the material, personal change and structural change belong together. As in the life of Jesus, being, doing and saying are at the heart of our integral task.[1]

The president of the Micah Network, Dr. Melba Maggay, is an accomplished writer and social anthropologist from the Philippines. She founded the Institute for Studies in Asian Church and Culture, and her books include *Transforming Society*,[2] which outlines a powerful evangelical case for social transformation, drawing from her own experience as a leader in mobilizing evangelicals in the "people's power" movement that overthrew the Marcos regime. Disregarding the artificial lines between "evangelical" and "ecumenical" originating historically in the United States, Dr. Maggay has been active as a speaker and board member in various NGO's and faith-based organizations dealing with religion and sustainable development.

Examples of leaders like this now proliferate in the Global South. They are rooted in social realities that make a version of Christian faith that is bifurcated and divided between those emphasizing evangelism and those advocating social justice irrelevant to their context. Further, their numbers, their books, their institutes, and their followers are all growing.

Of course, in the chaotic complexity of the emerging church in the Global South, it's possible to find examples of all forms of novel theological and practical expressions of Christian faith. Charlatans lead spiritual escapist movements that function more like cults. Many prosperity gospel preachers consistently reap the largest prosperity for themselves rather than their impoverished followers. Self-proclaimed prophets function like near-deities with mythic powers over their parishioners. Freedom from the domination of Western theology, institutional power, and money gives rise to a wide spectrum of faith expressions growing in diverse cultures.

Therefore, simplistic generalizations about the forms of faith emerging in the new majority contexts of world Christianity are impossible. But some assertions can be made, and then tested. Holistic expressions of the gospel, also called integral mission, seem to take root more naturally in these non-Western cultures. The entrenched Western patterns of institutionalized divisions that segregate the personal from the social dimensions of faith make far less sense in these contexts. Irrigating land sustainably with windmills, planting churches, and halting wife-beating feel more like organic parts of one whole.

It's undeniable that a major shift has also been occurring within sectors of US Christianity to transcend the dichotomy of faith that they originated, institutionalized, and then exported. Forty years ago, I worked with Senator Mark O. Hatfield, on whose staff I was serving, to write *Between a Rock and a Hard Place*.[3] It was Senator Hatfield's attempt to spell out, in considerable detail, how his evangelically rooted Christian faith intersected with the issues of war and peace, civil religion, poverty, the environment, and global hunger.

> Holistic expressions of the gospel, also called integral mission, seem to take root more naturally in these non-Western cultures.

What made the book notable was that it was so rare. Richard Ostling, who was *Time*'s religion correspondent during those days, called me to talk about the book after its publication. He was considering naming it *Time*'s Religion Book of the Year. The reason was that it was so rare to find an evangelical, much less a highly regarded elected official, speaking so clearly about the issues of justice and peace. (Ostling eventually selected Charles Colson's *Born Again*, written after Watergate and Colson's conversion but epitomizing the personal rather than the social dimension of faith.)

Filling the Theological Ditch

The decades since then have seen a cascade of books dealing with the relationship of Christian faith to issues of justice, peace, and care of creation. Many have come from evangelical authors and theologians who have rejected the claims of the religious Right and made the case in a variety of ways for the biblical call to care for the poor, preserve the creation, protect immigrants, and seek peace. Fewer, yet growing numbers of Pentecostal authors have joined this chorus. Meanwhile, biblical scholarship, often led by more mainline as well as Catholic theologians, has uncovered deeper layers of the social, political, and economic contexts impacting the experience of the Hebrew people, the setting for Jesus's ministry, and the rise of the early church. All this points toward the affirmation of both evangelism and social justice as parts of the gospel, rather than a binary choice between them.

However, an implicit dualism often remains. These two parts often remain siloed, both theologically and in practice. For many evangelicals, the focus remains on converting people to faith in Christ. Separately, they agree today that the Bible calls Christians to be concerned about the poor, and they are glad to serve in a soup kitchen or participate in other ministries of compassion. Fewer move beyond compassion to engage in direct advocacy for policies and political actions shaped by a commitment to social justice, although that number consistently grows.

Progressive liberal Christians, on the other hand, show a growing interest in forms of inward spirituality addressing the personal dimension of faith, and acknowledge the capacity of

God's Spirit to transform lives. But that often remains segregated from their passionate commitment to participate meaningfully in social action driven primarily by a liberal political agenda. While both groups are more likely to recognize that evangelism and social justice are two sides of the same coin, the emphasis in practice seems to be on the two separate sides.

This poses a basic theological challenge. My conviction is that this entire dichotomous framework is wrong and can never be resolved by a "both-and" instead of an "either-or" approach. A whole new starting point and a fresh paradigm are required. US Christianity has dug the church into a theological ditch over the last century. We can't climb out of it by trying to hold onto both sides. Rather, we must fill it in and start anew.

The most fundamental problem is that faith in Jesus Christ has been conceived as an individualistic experience that is separate from the world. God's work of salvation in this paradigm is directed only toward individuals, as if they lived in isolation from their social context. None of this would have been possible without the Enlightenment and Western cultural assumptions that placed the individual at the center of social, cultural, and political life. Extending this to religious life seemed natural, as we explored extensively in chapter 6.

Creating a version of faith focused exclusively on one's individual spiritual experience, assuming that God's work takes place in the "hearts" of individual persons rather than in the world, built a wall between these Christians and the life of the world. Their conviction was that the "world" (and the biblical meanings of this term were widely misunderstood) was headed for destruction, consumed by sin and death. Salvation meant saving oneself from the world. Christian life and practice constructed around separation from an evil world was the understandable result.

It's no wonder, then, that the modernist, social gospel tradition focused on the difference Christian faith could make for the common good of society. The church, essentially, could serve to give its members courage to do good, and they could make a difference in a progressive march toward justice. But just as evangelicals accepted secular assumptions about the primacy of the individual, liberals accepted secular assumptions about materialist and rationalistic understandings of social reality. Reacting against shallow, fundamentalist forms of piety that confined God's Spirit to emotional expressions of individualistic experience, they de-emphasized spirituality in general, trusting more in the rationality of committed social action with a faith in progress.

What Does God Love?

The foundational theological question to reframe our approach is this: What does God love? And how?

When we begin with the conviction that God's love is directed toward and found within all that God has created, everything changes. And frankly, it's hard to find a starting point that is more biblical. Even after the story of the flood in Genesis, God's covenantal love embraces every living thing and all that God has created. God's covenant is with the earth, and the rainbow reminds us continually of that promise (Gen 9:8–17).

Moreover, this love is not some separate and distant force field but rather animates and upholds all that God has created (Psalm 104). This is where we begin.

The presence of this all-embracing love does not ignore the ambiguity and potential for evil within the creation. Rather, it persists in the face of this, inviting us to a deep acceptance, knowing that the continual process of transformation comes through emptying and filling, through suffering and healing, through death and resurrection. This is woven into the life-giving fabric of creation and discovered from a depth of spiritual experience. It easily seems, to our normal Western way of thinking, that it's a contradiction for God's love to uphold "all things" in a world also harboring evil. But there's a reality embedded deep beneath the surface of things in which we can root our own life. Annie Dillard puts it this way:

> In the deeps are the violence and terror of which psychology has warned us. But if you ride these monsters deeper down, if you drop with them farther over the world's rim, you find what our sciences cannot locate or name, the substrate, the ocean or matrix or ether which buoys the rest, which gives goodness its power for good, and evil its power for evil, the unified field: our complex and inexplicable caring for each other, and for our life together here. This is given. It is not learned.[4]

In Ephesians, we read the prayer and the plea "to be strengthened in your inner being with power through his Spirit, and that Christ my dwell in your hearts through faith as you are being rooted and ground in love" (Eph 3:16b–17). But Paul goes on to explain the only way that can happen: "I pray that you may have the power to comprehend, with all the saints, what is the breadth and length and height and depth, and to know the love of Christ that surpasses knowledge, so that you may be filled with all the fullness of God" (Eph 3:18–19).

This is the key. The inner experience of Christ's presence through the Spirit connects us to a cosmic reality. The presence of God's love, upholding all that is, lies completely beyond our rational understanding. Yet we can experience this in intimately personal ways that unite us to a love embracing the whole creation. This spiritual reality destroys all our attempts at dualistic, binary ways of understanding our faith and reality itself.

> God's love is in the ongoing process of saving the world. This is the love that grasps us. It was displayed most fully and completely for all time and eternity in Jesus Christ.

God's love is in the ongoing process of saving the world. This is the love that grasps us. It was displayed most fully and completely for all time and eternity in Jesus Christ. When it touches and claims us, we are led through the life-giving process of death and resurrection. Our transformation is subsumed in the cosmic process of the world's salvation. In this fashion, our lives and the communities that are the source of shared strength and sustenance, of bread and wine, become the vehicles for the concrete social transformation of the context where we live and breathe. We participate in God's work of saving the world.

These perspectives are not new or original. They've simply been ignored by much of modern Western Christian thought, whether evangelical or liberal. They are found in the contemplative tradition, where the depth of the inward spiritual journey discovers hidden connections to the oceans of God's all-embracing love. This never comes without pain, suffering, and desolation. The "dark night of the soul" described by Saint John of the Cross and experienced by so many mystics is an essential part of the journey. It leads to the death of the "false self" and the discovery of resting in nothing more, or less, than the unfathomable love of God, which is sustaining, renewing, and saving the whole world.

Theology in the tradition of the Orthodox church, finding its roots in the church fathers of early Christianity, obviously developed far before, and remained separate from, the framing of Christian faith through the assumptions of Western culture and the Enlightenment. In Orthodox understanding, God's salvation is always directed toward the whole world, or creation. In the incarnation, God took on the flesh and blood of the creation in Jesus Christ. His life, death, and resurrection redeem the whole creation, overcoming the powers of evil and restoring its broken relationship to the Creator. The church lives within the spiritual power of this hope. Quoting again my late Orthodox and ecumenical friend Paulos Mar Gregorios, "Human redemption is inseparable from the redemption of time and space as well as of 'things.'"[5]

Similar theological perspectives have found their way into Protestant thought, although far from being mainstream. Notions of a cosmic Christology were central to Lutheran theologian Joseph Sittler's address to the WCC Assembly in New Delhi in 1961. Often this address is cited as a pivotal point for introducing these views to the wider church. Drawing on Orthodox insights long neglected, Sittler employed Colossians 1:15–20 as the biblical foundation for a cosmic vision of God's redemptive work in Christ that should underlie the call to unity and sociopolitical engagement in the world.[6]

Non-Western Wisdom

While some attention has been given to these perspectives in Western theology, and particularly by those working to create a compelling connection between Christianity and ecology (also a strong emphasis of Sittler), it's of interest to note where these views find expression in the non-Western church. Consider China, for example. The late bishop K. H. Ting, longtime leader of the government-sanctioned Chinese church and the China Christian Council, utilized a cosmic Christology in his attempts to forge a sociopolitical theology within that complex context. But more interesting was the work of the Chinese evangelical theologian Wang Weifan, a colleague of Ting's at Nanjing Union Theological Seminary. Describing Jesus as "not just the personal Savior of a few" but also the "Lord of the cosmos," Wang Weifan pointed to the "generative nature of God" ongoing in creation and related to the mystical nature of the encounter with Christ.[7] These ideas find resonance within elements of Chinese culture.

God loves the world and all that God has created. God's generative, redemptive presence continues within creation, marking its foundation and forecasting its future. We can touch and be grasped by the power of this love. It is closer to us than we are to ourselves. We have seen what this looks like in Jesus, and we are invited to be "in Christ" and united with those in a worshipping community. There, we celebrate at table and font the continuing, transforming power of God's Spirit, and we taste and participate in God's salvation of the world.

The fresh expressions of such ancient faith are more likely to find fertile soil in the non-Western cultures that are the context for Christianity's future, already taking shape. The signs and examples are plentiful. As Christian faith grows not only wider but also deeper in these settings, it is forging understandings of discipleship and faith formation free from the absurdities of an evangelical versus a social gospel. In so doing, it is drawing creatively on indigenous cultural resources, while engaging in the creative dialogue between gospel and culture that is a mark of a growing, vital church.

In an evangelical community development project in Kerala, in a thriving indigenous Pentecostal Church in the slums of Jakarta, in a growing Orthodox community drawing richly on its tribal culture in Kenya, in a Catholic mass with charismatic worship in Sao Paulo, in an ecumenical seminary responding to new church growth in Cuba, in an African immigrant congregation providing assistance to victims of Hurricane Harvey in

Houston, and in thousands of places like these, we glimpse the future of faith.

A gospel that roots followers of Jesus in God's unfathomable, cosmic love as it engages them in God's salvation of the world provides a trajectory for US congregations as well. When I talk with those researching the precipitous decline of participation by millennials (and those even younger) in the church today, the word I hear most often is "indifference." Surveys show that it's not a case of these people becoming atheists, rejecting any notion of God or spiritual reality. Rather, they have become callously indifferent to the presence of the church.

When asked why, responses vary. But in most cases, such people have concluded that the church is indifferent to the world. Further, it's not just a soup kitchen or walk for hunger that will change that perception. Those who disregard America's 350,000 congregations, in general, reject churches who reject others. They are turned off by self-righteous judgment. They don't see deeds that match words. They smell marketing strategies rather than authentic relationships. The don't find loving communities among those who preach about loving their neighbors. And they fail to see a spiritually rooted vision of personal and social transformation.

In the United States as well as in world Christianity, congregations creating the future of faith will understand and demonstrate that the gospel isn't real if it isn't making a difference for good in the specific social context where it is placed. Jesus was God incarnate, in flesh and blood, at a place and time to be seen and known as God's radical love. So must Christ's body, the church, be. As a community, it becomes the gathering of those who participate together in the transformation of their lives by God's grace in order to take part in God's ongoing, redemptive work in creation. *Future faith will be marked by followers of Jesus who are grasped by a love that compels their participation in God's salvation of this world.*

DISCUSSION GUIDE

CHALLENGE ONE: REVITALIZING WITHERING
CONGREGATIONS

1. What one word or phrase would you use to describe your faith community or congregation? Do you see the description as positive or negative (or neither)? Why?

2. The author cites statistics that point to a decline in people attending both mainline and some evangelical church denominations? Has your faith community experienced such decline? If so, why? If not, why not?

3. In contrast, many faith communities across the world are growing. What does the author suggest the North American church can learn from these vibrant and growing communities of faith?

4. What example of the growing global church provided in the chapter was particularly striking to you? Why?

5. What more do you want to learn or do based on reading this chapter of the book?

CHALLENGE TWO: EMBRACING THE COLOR OF THE FUTURE

1. What is a "None"? Do you know any? How has your faith community talked about the "Nones"?

2. Why does the author suggest that denominations and faith communities focus on being more multiracially diverse and aware?

3. What strategies or examples of racial diversity did the author provide? In what ways do these examples help or encourage your own faith community to become more racially diverse?

4. What is your reaction to the author's statement that "the North American church must embrace the changing color of its future with its decisive shift in its dynamics of power"? If you agree with the statement, what might that mean for your faith community now and in the future?

5. What more do you want to learn or do based on reading this chapter of the book?

CHALLENGE THREE: SEEING THROUGH NON-WESTERN EYES

1. What major shifts in the church does the author describe in this chapter?

2. How would you define the word *paradigm*? What has been the prevailing paradigm in your faith community? Why might you wish to change this prevailing paradigm? Or not?

3. The author describes one important shift as seeing the world through a different set of lenses. What examples of these lenses does he provide? Which of these examples was particularly striking to you? Why?

4. Why does the author say we are at a "hinge point" in the history of global Christianity? From that hinge point, how does the author see the future?

5. What is your reaction to the author's discussion of seeing through Native American or Indigenous Peoples' lenses? How can you or your faith community benefit from these perspectives?

6. What more do you want to learn or do based on reading this chapter of the book?

CHALLENGE FOUR: PERCEIVING THE WORLD AS SACRED

1. What historical developments in both society and the church have had an impact on how we view the sacred or holy in our modern world?

2. How do you respond to this quote by Larry Rasmussen: "Rich though we be as consumers, as creatures who belong body and soul to the cosmos we are paupers"? Do you agree that creation has been compromised by modern human action? Why or why not?

3. To what voices or perspectives does the author suggest we pay close attention? Why?

4. How would you complete this statement: The created world is _____.

5. What more do you want to learn or do based on reading this chapter of the book?

CHALLENGE FIVE: AFFIRMING SPIRIT-FILLED COMMUNITIES

1. When you hear the term *spirit-filled communities* what do you envision? In what ways is your faith community spirit-filled? In what ways is it not?

2. What did you learn about Pentecostal communities in this chapter? What example or perspective stood out for you? Why?

3. In what ways does the author say that Pentecostal communities of faith sometimes live within a bubble, insulated from other Christian communities?

4. One critique of Pentecostalism is that it focuses on experience but is lacking in good theology, and even disdains academic theology. What is true about this critique? How is this changing?

5. What can be gained by "recognizing and affirming the spirit-filled gifts of the global Pentecostal world"?

6. What more do you want to learn or do based on reading this chapter of the book?

CHALLENGE SIX: REJECTING THE HERESY OF INDIVIDUALISM

1. What do you think of Jean Vanier's proposal that for any community to thrive, "there must be more members who can say 'me for the community' than those who say 'the community for me'"?

2. How does the world around us, and sometimes even the church, organize life with "me" at the center?

3. From what biblical examples does the author draw in the perspective of life organized around community? What benefits are experienced "in community"?

4. How does God's nature itself lead us toward community?

5. What examples of both individualistic ministry and community-based ministry are given in the chapter?

6. How can the power and promise of grounding faith in community, which is so prevalent in global Christianity, sharpen your faith community's life together?

7. What more do you want to learn or do based on reading this chapter of the book?

CHALLENGE SEVEN: DE-AMERICANIZING THE GOSPEL

1. The author expresses some strong political perspectives in this chapter. What is your initial reaction to what is said?

2. How or why has the focus on social action in the church sometimes run into opposition? How has this struggle spilled over into American politics? Do you agree or disagree with the author's perspective on this? Why?

3. When the author says that "the white religious bubble in America is about to burst," to what circumstances does he point? Do you agree or disagree with this perspective? Why? How might or could this bursting bubble impact your community of faith?

4. What steps does the author suggest be taken in order to de-Americanize the gospel? Which of these steps might you say is most important? Why?

5. In this chapter, the line separating faith and politics is crossed and erased, challenged and pushed. What do you think about this? What key learning do you take away from this chapter?

6. What more do you want to learn or do based on reading this chapter of the book?

CHALLENGE EIGHT: DEFEATING DIVISIVE CULTURE WARS

1. What are some of the subjects that have been divisive, both in culture and in the church? What examples does the author give?

2. In what ways are the global church and some faith communities in the Global North and West not in agreement on certain cultural perspectives? How does that affect the way we interact in the church?

3. The author suggests that defeating divisive wars in the life of the church is imperative if world Christianity will have a vital future. Do you agree or disagree with this? Why?

4. In what ways does the author suggest we must be "honest" as we work on breaking down barriers to Christian fellowship?

5. How and where do we find common ground, even as we hold differing views? What is the most important thing or belief that holds us all together as Christians?

6. What more do you want to learn or do based on reading this chapter of the book?

CHALLENGE NINE: BELONGING BEFORE BELIEVING

1. What do you think of the idea that in our modern culture people are working and consuming on their own terms more and more? What examples of this does the author give? How have you experienced this?

2. In what ways does this widening of individual choice have an effect on the organized church? In what ways is the church responding?

3. How has the explosion of groups, initiatives, and organizations in the global faith community led to a kind of chaos? What changes are needed to bring some order to the chaos?

4. What is your reaction to the story the author tells about Alysha? Does it ring true for you? Do you think it is a common experience for many in faith communities?

5. What is more important—belonging or believing? Why? In your experience does one usually precede the other? If so, in what way? Name some examples.

6. What do you think of the author's statement that nurturing faith in the future will be driven more by relational connections (how one belongs) than by doctrinal understandings (what one believes)?

7. What more do you want to learn or do based on reading this chapter of the book?

CHALLENGE TEN: SAVING *THIS* WORLD

1. The author begins this chapter with an example of Christian mission in a culture that did not know of the gospel. What important conclusions came out of this example? The author lists "three salient features" that arise from the story. How do you summarize these features? Do these conclusions make sense to you? Why or why not?

2. What "divide" in the Western church does the author describe? In what ways have you experienced this divide? How has this divide sometimes spilled over into the church in the Global South?

3. Where does the author find hopeful signs that the divide can be overcome?

4. The author identifies a key foundational theological question as "What does God love? And how?" How does the author

answer these questions using scriptural examples and other sources?

5. Where does the author see creative expressions of embodying God's love in the global church?

6. What is your response to the author's statement that "congregations creating the future of faith will understand and demonstrate that the gospel isn't real if it isn't making a difference for good in the specific context where it is placed"?

7. After reading this book what "marks" will or should define faith communities in the future? How will your faith community embody these marks?

NOTES

CHAPTER 1: REVITALIZING WITHERING CONGREGATIONS

1. David A. Roozen, "American Congregations 2015: Thriving and Surviving," Hartford Institute for Religion Research, 2016, 2, https://tinyurl.com/y9a5s6z3.
2. Roozen, "American Congregations 2015," 2.
3. "America's Changing Religious Landscape," Pew Research Center, May 12, 2015, https://tinyurl.com/y9hye3fk.
4. Melissa Binder, "Yes, Portland Is America's Most Religiously Unaffiliated Metro. But Who Exactly Are the Nones?," *The Oregonian /Oregon Live*, March 18, 2015, https://tinyurl.com/ycj5e8ot.
5. "America's Changing Religious Landscape," Pew Research Center.
6. Roozen, "American Congregations 2015," 13.
7. Roozen, "American Congregations 2015," 4.
8. Roozen, "American Congregations 2015," 15.
9. Warren Bird and Scott Thumma, "A New Decade of Megachurches: 2011 Profile of Large Attendance Churches in the United States," Leadership Network and Hartford Institute for Religious Research, November 22, 2011, https://tinyurl.com/y7ts5sqk.
10. Todd M. Johnson and Kenneth R. Ross, *Atlas of Global Christianity: 1910–2010* (Edinburgh: Edinburgh University Press, 2009).
11. "Christianity in Its Global Context, 1970–2020: Society, Religion, and Mission," Center for the Study of Global Christianity,

Gordon-Conwell Theological Seminary, June 2013, https://tinyurl
.com/y9hxhxgk.

CHAPTER 2: EMBRACING THE COLOR OF THE FUTURE

1. "America's Changing Religious Landscape," Pew Research Center,
   May 12, 2015, https://tinyurl.com/y9hye3fk.
2. "America's Changing Religious Landscape," Pew Research Center.
3. Darrin J. Rogers, "Assemblies of God 2014 Statistics Released,
   Reveals Ethnic Transformation," Flower Pentecostal Heritage
   Center, June 18, 2015, https://tinyurl.com/yagj68kx.
4. Michael Lipka, "The Most and Least Racially Diverse U.S. Religious Groups," Pew Research Center, July 27, 2015, https://
   tinyurl.com/y93d9me9.
5. Robert P. Jones, "The Changing American Landscape" (presentation, Fifth Annual President's Interfaith and Community Service Campus Challenge, Washington, DC, September 10, 2015),
   https://tinyurl.com/yd93mzom.
6. Jones, "The Changing American Landscape."
7. Jones, "The Changing American Landscape."
8. Hosffman Ospino, "Hispanic Ministry in Catholic Parishes: A
   Summary Report of Findings from the *National Study of Catholic Parishes with Hispanic Ministry*," Boston College, School of
   Theology and Ministry, 2014, 8, https://tinyurl.com/yc9we9kf.
   This study was done in collaboration with The Center for Applied
   Research in the Apostolate (CARA) at Georgetown University.
   While the Pew study put this estimate at 33 percent, the information from this study, supported by CARA and based on actual
   reporting from parishes, is probably more accurate, with the percentage at 38–40 percent and growing.
9. Ospino, "Hispanic Ministry," 7.
10. Full information about Convergence, including its commitments,
    board of directors, events, and plans can be found at its website:
    convergenceus.org.
11. "Initiatives," Convergence, https://tinyurl.com/y7zn846d.

12. David A. Roozen, "American Congregations 2015: Thriving and Surviving," Hartford Institute for Religion Research, 2016, 1, https://tinyurl.com/y9a5s6z3.

13. Roozen, "American Congregations 2015," 6.

CHAPTER 3: SEEING THROUGH NON-WESTERN EYES

1. Charles Taylor, *A Secular Age* (Cambridge, MA: Belknap Press of Harvard University Press, 2007).

2. James K. A. Smith, *How (Not) to Be Secular: Reading Charles Taylor* (Grand Rapids: Eerdmans, 2014)

3. Tim Stafford, "Historian Ahead of His Time," *Christianity Today*, February 8, 2007, https://tinyurl.com/23omegd.

4. Andrew F. Walls, "Eusebius Tries Again: The Task of Reconceiving and Re-Visioning the Study of Christian History," in *Enlarging the Story: Perspectives on Writing World Christian History*, ed. Wilbert R. Shenk (Maryknoll, NY: Orbis, 2002), 1.

5. Wesley Granberg-Michaelson, *From Times Square to Timbuktu: The Post-Christian West Meets the Non-Western Church* (Grand Rapids: Eerdmans, 2013), 137–41.

6. Granberg-Michaelson, *From Times Square*, 154. I'm offering here my recollections of this conversation, based on notes and my own interpretation, and not attributing these phrases directly to Professor Walls. A full account of my time in Ghana is found in the epilogue to *From Times Square*, 153–61.

7. Richard Twiss, *One Nation, Many Tribes* (Minneapolis: Chosen, 2000).

8. Richard Twiss, *Rescuing the Gospel from the Cowboys: A Native American Expression of the Jesus Way* (Downers Grove, IL: InterVarsity, 2015), 15–16.

9. Twiss, *Rescuing the Gospel*, 12.

10. Joseph Epes Brown, ed., *The Sacred Pipe: Black Elk's Account of the Seven Rites of the Oglala Sioux* (Norman: University of Oklahoma Press, 1953)

11. Kaitlin B. Curtice, *Glory Happening: Finding the Divine in Everyday Places* (Brewster, Massachusetts: Paraclet Press, 2017)

12. Patrick J. Twohy, *Finding a Way Home: Indian and Catholic Spiritual Paths of the Plateau Tribes*, 5th ed. (n.p.: Patrick J. Twohy, 2009).

13. Owen Barfield, *Saving the Appearances* (New York: Harcourt Brace Jovanovich, 1965), 78.

CHAPTER 4: PERCEIVING THE WORLD AS SACRED

1. "An Appendix," in "The Directory for the Publick Worship of God," Center for Reformed Theology and Apologetics, https://tinyurl.com/y8u6b9kr.

2. "An Appendix."

3. Preface of "The Directory for the Publick Worship of God," Center for Reformed Theology and Apologetics, https://tinyurl.com/yc74x52h.

4. Gregg A. Mast, "An Elegant Book," *Reformed Review* 52, no. 3 (April 1999): 283.

5. Note should be made of differences in Luther's views, who saw the presence of Christ's body and blood "in, with and under" the bread and wine, and whose churches typically maintained various expressions of liturgical art and practice.

6. Carolyn Merchant, *The Death of Nature: Women, Ecology, and the Scientific Revolution* (San Francisco: Harper & Row, 1980), 169.

7. Max Weber, *The Protestant Ethic and the Spirit of Capitalism* (New York: Scribner, 1958), 178.

8. Larry Rasmussen, "Whence Climate Injustice," in *A Companion to Public Theology*, ed. Sebastian Kim and Katie Day (Leiden: Brill, 2017), 349.

9. Paulos Mar Gregorios, *The Human Presence: An Orthodox View of Nature* (Geneva: World Council of Churches, 1978).

10. Paulos Mar Gregorios, "New Testament Foundations for Understanding the Creation," in *Tending the Garden: Essays on the Gospel and the Earth*, ed. Wesley Granberg-Michaelson (Grand Rapids: Eerdmans, 1987), 85.

11. Gregorios, "New Testament Foundations," 90.

12. Writings on orthodox views of creation, ecology, and environment are plentiful. Ecumenical discussions, including those by the WCC, have given needed visibility to orthodox perspectives, such as Gennadios Limouris, ed., *Justice Peace and Integrity of Creation: Insights from Orthodoxy* (Geneva: World Council of Churches, 1990). A good overview, drawing on ancient orthodox sources, is Elizabeth Theokritoff, *Living in God's Creation: Orthodox Perspectives on Ecology* (Crestwood, NY: St. Vladimir's Seminary Press, 2009).

13. From Richard Rohr, "Great Chain of Being," Center for Action and Contemplation, November 13, 2016, https://tinyurl.com/y8vyczer. Reference is from Bonaventure, *Bonaventure: The Soul's Journey to God*, trans. Ewert H. Cousins (Ramsey, NJ: Paulist, 1978), 100–101 (5.8).

14. Francis, *Laudato Si': On Care for Our Common Home*, May 24, 2015, §115, https://tinyurl.com/yb5zqay8. The quote within this paragraph of the encyclical is from Romano Guardini, *The End of the Modern World* (Wilmington, DE: ISI Books, 1998), 55.

15. Francis, *Laudato Si'*, §217.

16. Francis, *Laudato Si'*, §217.

17. Francis, *Laudato Si'*, §246.

18. My first book on the subject was *A Worldly Spirituality: The Call to Take Care of the Earth* (San Francisco: Harper & Row 1984). It attempted to develop a biblical and theological mandate for environmental care. *Tending the Garden: Essays on the Gospel and the Earth*, previously mentioned, which I edited, was a collection of presentations given at one of the conferences at the Au Sable Institute of Environmental Studies and includes contributions from Loren Wilkinson, Mary Evelyn Jegen, Larry Rasmussen, Paulos Mar Gregorios, and others. In 1988 I wrote *Ecology and Life: Accepting Our Environmental Responsibility* (Waco, TX: Word, 1988), which was part of a series of books on issues of Christian conscience, edited by Vernon Grounds.

19. An extensive, comprehensive bibliography of books on Christianity and ecology was compiled by Peter Bakken of the Au Sable Institute of Environmental Studies and can be found at the website

of the Yale Forum on Religion and Ecology at https://tinyurl.com/
yc6auklc. This bibliography, the most exhaustive that I have read,
is in three parts and has annotated comments on each of its hundreds of works, through 2014.

20. Sallie McFague, *The Body of God: An Ecological Theology* (Minneapolis: Fortress Press, 1993).

21. From Richard Rohr, "God In All Things," Center for Action and
Contemplation, October 23, 2016, https://tinyurl.com/y8xy6gyf.

22. Ilia Delio, *The Unbearable Wholeness of Being: God, Evolution,
and the Power of Love* (Maryknoll, NY: Orbis, 2013), 79.

CHAPTER 5: AFFIRMING SPIRIT-FILLED COMMUNITIES

1. Marshall Allen, "Pentecostal Movement Celebrates Humble
Roots," *Washington Post*, April 15, 2006, https://tinyurl.com
/y8acy3cy.

2. Ivan Satyavrata, "The Feeding of 10,000," *Sojourners*, January
2017, 37.

3. Wonsuk Ma, "When the Spirit Comes Down," *Sojourners*, January
2017, 38.

4. Ma, "When the Spirit," 32–38. He also draws attention to the
work of Donald E. Miller and Tetsunao Yamamori, authors of
*Global Pentecostalism: The New Face of Christian Social Engage-
ment* (Berkeley: University of California Press, 2007). I gave careful attention to their work in *From Times Square to Timbuktu: The
Post-Christian West Meets the Non-Western Church* (Grand Rapid:
Eerdmans, 2013), 142–45.

5. Todd M. Johnson and Kenneth R. Ross, eds., *Atlas of Global
Christianity: 1910–2010* (Edinburgh: Edinburgh University Press,
2009), 100.

6. From Richard Rohr, "Experiential Knowledge," Center for
Action and Contemplation, January 25, 2017, https://tinyurl.com
/yaj73233.

7. Daniel Castelo, *Pentecostalism as a Christian Mystical Tradition*
(Grand Rapids: Eerdmans, 2017). Castelo thoughtfully explores
these connections in this new book.

8. Brad Brooks, "Fight for Growing Pentecostal Vote in Brazil," Associated Press, September 30, 2014, https://tinyurl.com/y9vajzf9.
9. See interview with Donald E. Miller in Micael Grenholm, "Why Most Pentecostals Around the World Are Progressive," Pax Pneuma, January 28, 2017, https://tinyurl.com/y99k9jhs.

CHAPTER 6: REJECTING THE HERESY OF INDIVIDUALISM

1. John Dewey, "The Ethics of Democracy," in *The Early Works of John Dewey, Volume 1, 1882–1898: Early Essays and Leibniz's New Essays, 1882–1888*, ed. Jo Ann Boydston and George E. Axetell (Carbondale: Southern Illinois University Press, 2008), 232.
2. Richard Wike, "5 Ways Americans and Europeans Are Different," Pew Research Center, April 19, 2016, https://tinyurl.com/ya9p89f3.
3. Dan M. Kahan, Hank Jenkins-Smith, and Donald Braman, "Cultural Cognition of Scientific Consensus," *Journal of Risk Research* 14, no. 2 (2011): 147–74.
4. Dietrich Bonhoeffer, *Life Together* (New York: Harper & Row, 1954).
5. Dietrich Bonhoeffer, *Letters and Papers from Prison*, Dietrich Bonhoeffer Works 8 (Minneapolis: Fortress Press, 2010), 467.
6. Richard Rohr, *Divine Dance: The Trinity and Your Transformation* (New Kensington, PA: Whitaker House, 2017). See also Cynthia Bourgeault, *The Holy Trinity and the Law of Three: Discovering the Radical Truth at the Heart of Christianity* (Boulder, Colorado: Shambhala Publications, 2013)
7. Richard Rohr, "A Circle Dance," Center for Action and Contemplation, February 27, 2017, https://tinyurl.com/y7fqgb3y.
8. Richard Rohr, "Inner and Outer Worlds Converge," Center for Action and Contemplation, March 2, 2017, https://tinyurl.com/yd483lhd.
9. Michael C. Mack, "The Pioneers of the Small-Group Movement," *Christianity Today*, July 24, 2014, https://tinyurl.com/ya4fn-qyxonline. This article, based in part on an interview with Lyman

Coleman, provides a helpful picture of how the small-group movement originated.

10. Michael Onyebuchi Eze, *Intellectual History in Contemporary South Africa* (London: Palgrave McMillian, 2010), 190–91. See also "John Samuel Mbiti's Response to Wesley Granberg-Michaelson's Lecture," video, 1:24:45, uploaded by Jonathan J. Armstrong, September 3, 2014, https://tinyurl.com/y9z9osh6.

CHAPTER 7: DE-AMERICANIZING THE GOSPEL

1. From INFEMIT's mission statement found on their website: https://tinyurl.com/y924pmw9.
2. The entire statement, with its original signers and comments, can be accessed on the INFEMIT website at http://tinyurl.com/ybjfyst8.
3. Francis FitzGerald, *The Evangelicals: The Struggle to Shape America* (New York: Simon & Schuster, 2017), 536. FitzGerald's book is a thoroughly researched, comprehensive history of evangelicals in America, and the chapters "The New Evangelicals" and "The Transformation of the Christian Right" provide a compelling narrative of developments through the time of Obama's presidency.
4. FitzGerald, *The Evangelicals*, 579.
5. FitzGerald, *The Evangelicals*, 583.
6. FitzGerald, *The Evangelicals*, 610.
7. "The Shifting Religious Identity of Latinos in the United States," Pew Research Center, May 7, 2014, http://tinyurl.com/y9jrzt45.
8. Thomas Wood, "Racism Motived Trump Voters More Than Authoritarianism," *The Washington Post*, April 17, 2017, http://tinyurl.com/ybotswzy.
9. Tom Krattenmaker, "The Key to Understanding Evangelicals' Upside-Down Support for the Travel Ban," Religion News Service, March 3, 2017, http://tinyurl.com/y7wb2c2d.
10. Robert P. Jones, *The End of White Christian America* (New York: Simon & Schuster, 2016). This recent book by the CEO of the Public Religion Research Institute documents all these trends.

11. Lisa Cannon Green, "Americans Optimistic about America's Future; Most Say U.S. Has Special Bond with God," Lifeway Research, July 1, 2015, http://tinyurl.com/y7hdj42h.
12. Lauren Markoe, "White Evangelicals, Catholics and Mormons Carried Trump," Religion News Service, November 9, 2016, http://tinyurl.com/ya9neom9.
13. "A Declaration of American Evangelicals Concerning Donald Trump," with its original seventy-five signers, can be accessed on the Change.org website, http://tinyurl.com/zttqjr7.
14. Sarah Posner, "The Religious Right Is Steeling Itself for a Biblical Battle on Trump's Behalf," *The Washington Post*, March 6, 2017, http://tinyurl.com/ycj4jpjd.
15. Jim Wallis, "Post-American Christianity," *The Post-American*, Fall 1971, http://tinyurl.com/y933ptxa.
16. Rod Dreher, *The Benedict Option: A Strategy for Christians in a Post-Christian Nation* (New York: Sentinel, 2017).
17. Pope John Paul II, *Sollicitudo Rei Socialis*, §38, https://tinyurl.com/y728zzpp.
18. For an example of what it looks like for Christians to stand in the gap following Charlottesville, Virginia, see Lisa Sharon Harper's blog, "After Charlottresville, the Question We Absolutely Have to Answer: Who is Willing to Take Up Their Cross?," at https://tinyurl.com/yatsl3cw

CHAPTER 8: DEFEATING DIVISIVE CULTURE WARS

1. This is from the text of Nadia Marcias's unpublished remarks at the WCRC General Council in Leipzig, Germany, on June 30, 2017.
2. John Mark N. Reynolds, "Is the PCUSA Still Christian?" *Patheos*, March 25, 2015, http://tinyurl.com/y7xswc3t.
3. See, for example, Caleb Owen, "Perspectives on Understanding Homosexuality and Homophobia in Africa," H-Net Humanities and Social Sciences Online, February 4, 2016, http://tinyurl.com/y7hzcpo8. This provides an introduction to the scholarship available.

4. The story of the Arlington Group's origin and focus on the Federal Marriage Amendment is recounted with illuminating historical detail by Francis FitzGerald, *The Evangelicals: The Struggle to Shape America* (New York: Simon & Schuster, 2017), 482–506.

5. An early example is Charles M. Olsen, *Transforming Church Boards into Communities of Spiritual Leaders* (Washington, DC: Alban Institute, 1995). This was followed by Danny E. Morris and Charles M. Olsen, *Discerning God's Will Together: A Spiritual Practice for the Church* (Nashville: Upper Room Books, 1997). The Uniting Church of Australia's important contribution, which was shared ecumenically, was first elaborated by Jill Tabart, *Coming to Consensus: A Case Study for the Churches* (Geneva: WCC Publications, 2003). Several books have followed since then, including Lon Fendall, Jan Wood, and Bruce Bishop, *Practicing Discernment Together: Finding God's Way Forward in Decision-Making* (Newberg, OR: Barclay, 2007); Ruth Haley Barton, *Pursuing God's Will Together: A Discernment Practice for Leadership Groups* (Downers Grove, IL: InterVarsity, 2012); and, more recently, Terence Corkin and Julia Kuhn Wallace, *The Church Guide for Making Decisions Together* (Nashville: Abingdon, 2017).

6. James Brownson, *Bible, Gender and Sexuality: Reframing the Church's Debate on Same-Sex Relationships* (Grand Rapids: Eerdmans, 2013). I was privileged to write the foreword for this book. It also contains extensive references to biblical scholarship dealing with this question. Later, this contribution appeared: Matthew Vines, *God and the Gay Christian: The Biblical Case in Support of Same-Sex Relationships* (New York: Convergent, 2014). Matthew Vines directs The Reformation Project, providing teaching and resources for promoting the full inclusion of LGBTQ persons in the life of the church. Numerous other books have been published as well as conservative-minded critiques in this ongoing discussion.

7. "Sexuality in Africa," special issue, *Journal of Theology for Southern Africa*, no. 155 (July 2016). This issue also contains the full text of the KwaZulu-Natal Declaration.

8. "Uganda Anti-Homosexuality Act, 2014," Wikipedia, http://tinyurl.com/n954so5. This provides an extensive discussion of the process leading to the adoption of this measure and its aftermath, with links to many sources.

9. Kapya Kaoma and Petronella Chalwe, "The Good Samaritan and Minorities in Africa: Christianity, the US Christian Right and the Dialogical Ethics of *Ubuntu*," *The Journal of Theology for Southern Africa*, no. 155 (July 2016): 195.

CHAPTER 9: BELONGING BEFORE BELIEVING

1. For an illuminating account of these developments, see Nathan Heller, "The Gig Is Up," *The New Yorker*, May 15, 2017, 52–63.

2. Heller, "The Gig Is Up," 54.

3. Robert Wuthnow, *Boundless Faith: The Global Outreach of American Churches* (Berkeley: University of California Press, 2009)

4. One of the most insightful authors identifying this trend has been Diana Butler Bass, *Christianity after Religion: The End of the Church and the Birth of a New Spiritual Awakening* (San Francisco: Harper One, 2012). See especially chapter 6, "Belonging" (pp. 169–98) and chapter 7, "The Great Reversal" (pp. 199–214).

5. Paul G. Hiebert, "How Much Must Papayya 'Know' about the Gospel to Be Converted?" Conversion, Culture, and Cognitive Categories, *Gospel in Context* 1, no. 4 (1978): 24–29, http://tinyurl.com/ybrq3euw. For another excellent explanation of these concepts applied to the church, see Paul Hiebert, "Sets and Structures: A Study of Church Patterns," in *New Horizons in World Mission: Evangelicals and Christian Mission in the 1980's*, ed. David J. Hesselgrave (Grand Rapids: Baker, 1980).

6. John Ortberg, "Category Confusion: Is the Question for Christians 'Out or In' or 'Farther or Closer?'," *Christianity Today*, June 2010, http://tinyurl.com/y7kfvxeo.

CHAPTER 10: SAVING *THIS* WORLD

1. "Integral Mission," Micah Network, http://tinyurl.com/ycmofpxd.
2. Melba Padilla Maggay, *Transforming Society* (Eugene, OR: Wipf & Stock, 2010).
3. Mark O. Hatfield, *Between a Rock and a Hard Place* (Waco, TX: Word, 1976). The single book that had perhaps the most influence on evangelical attitudes toward social justice in the 1970s was Ron Sider's *Rich Christians in an Age of Hunger* (Downers Grove, IL: InterVarsity, 1978). Several editions have sold more than four hundred thousand copies. A new and revised version was published by Thomas Nelson in 2005. Jim Wallis's first book, *Agenda for Biblical People* (New York: Harper & Row, 1976), also had considerable influence during this time as a unique voice on biblical faith and social justice.
4. Annie Dillard, *Teaching a Stone to Talk: Expeditions and Encounters* (New York: HarperPerennial, 2013), 19–20, quoted in Richard Rohr, "Cosmic Forgiveness," Center for Action and Contemplation, September 1, 2017, http://tinyurl.com/y9924jpb.
5. Paulos Gregorios, *The Human Presence: An Orthodox View of Nature* (Geneva: World Council of Churches, 1978), 81.
6. Joseph Sittler, "Called to Unity," *Ecumenical Review* 14 (January 1962): 177–87.
7. Andrew Chow, "Wang Weifan's Cosmic Christ," *Modern Theology* 32, no. 3 (July 2016): 384–96, http://tinyurl.com/ydhjudzy.

ACKNOWLEDGMENTS

While books are normally written by an individual, in truth they always emerge from a community of relationships, experiences, and ideas that make it possible. This is certainly the case with *Future Faith*.

My agent, Kathy Helmers, of the Creative Trust Literary Group, was indispensable in helping me focus the message of the book and then explore the best options for the publisher. Working with Fortress Press has been a gift. Scott Tunseth, my editor, has brought his professional expertise as well as his insightful personal attentiveness to this process. The whole team at Fortress Press has proven to be a reliable and trustworthy partner, for which I am deeply grateful.

Several friends have shared their expertise, reading over various parts of the manuscript and improving its content, including Larry Rasmussen, Reinhold Niebuhr Professor Emeritus of Christian Ethics at Union Theological Seminary. Larry and I now sing in the choir of our congregation, United Church of Santa Fe. Breaks in choir rehearsals were frequently absorbed in dialogue over this book. Wonsuk Ma, Distinguished Professor of Global Christianity at Oral Roberts University, shared his insights on the Pentecostal world and much more over dialogue while in Korea together and afterward, and has been a consistent supporter of this project.

Scott Thumma, director of the Hartford Institute for Religion Research, was generous in sharing insights into findings from their impressive congregational studies. Michael Adee, director of the Global Faith and Justice Project, contributed firsthand experience of his organization's pioneering work around issues of sexuality and religion in Africa and elsewhere.

Over breakfast at a diner in Chicago, Soong-Chan Rah, professor of church growth and evangelism at North Park Seminary, gladly accepted my request that he write the foreword for this book. His own work has explored similar avenues forecasting the future of faith for American Christianity. Jim Wallis, president and founder of *Sojourners* and a lifelong friend, was ceaseless in his encouragement for my writing and his support for this book's message.

My ecumenical experience among the diverse expressions of world Christianity continues to be my life's privilege and my heart's passion. Two decades of work with the Global Christian Forum, including with Huibert van Beek and Larry Miller, its past two secretaries, and its entire international committee, has opened countless portals of insight into Christianity's global journey. This built on the foundation of my previous work with the World Council of Churches and multiple enduring relationships. All that has enriched the stories and convictions of this book.

ACKNOWLEDGMENTS

My life's partner, wife, and best friend, Karin, has been the most wonderful person to accompany me throughout the process of conceiving, writing, and publishing this book. She has never doubted the importance of what I have wanted to share, nor the time and energy that this would take. I'm so grateful for our journey together.